AT SATAN'S ALTAR

AT SATAN'S ALTAR

A COLLECTION OF PRAYERS, CHANTS, AFFIRMATIONS, HYMNS, AND RITUALS

BY

MARIE RAVENSOUL

IN
SATAN'S
HONOUR
PRESS

Printed in Canada
First Edition, 2018

ISBN 978-1-7752624-0-4

Editing by Sephera Giron
Front Cover Image by Amanda MacNeil
Illustrations by:
     Amanda MacNeil (pp. 18, 40, 85, 109, & 121)
     Letitia Pfinder (pp. 66 & 167)
Book Design by V.I.M

In Satan's Honour Press
2336 Bloor Street W.
PO Box 84528
Toronto, Ontario
M6S 4Z7
Canada

www.In-Satans-Honour.com

This book is dedicated to Satan,
my Teacher, Lord, Muse,
Father, Master, and God.

And to R.J. Womack (Brother Nero),
my Friend, Mentor, and Priest.
Thank you for everything.

CONTENTS

INTRODUCTION

THIS book was written to honour Satan. The writings herein express my adoration for the Primordial One who goes by many names. Throughout the ages, many have called him Pan, the All-Begetter and the Horned God of the witches; others have called him Lucifer, the Light Bearer. Some call him Iblis, the pillar of fire, and then there is Melek Ta'us, the Peacock Angel of the Yezidis. I have called him by these names in this book, and touched on some of his many characteristics and manifestations. This is a celebration of Satan.

Since the beginning, Satan has encouraged humankind to become something greater. In all the religions, legends, beliefs, myths, and stories surrounding Satan throughout the ages, he has always been the bringer of enlightenment in some form or another. The symbol is different in each story, but whether it is a fruit or fire, the message is the same. When he approached the first woman, he invited her to know and then to become something great. He invites us to do the same. He invites us to know him.

Satan's wisdom has conquered the world, despite the resistance of some who have refused to embrace his message. It is because of him that humanity has an individual consciousness and a Will that is free to choose how to live. We have the ability to create and destroy, to love and hate, and to expand our knowledge. We have magick, literature, art, technology, medicine, science, philosophy, music, and mathematics because Satan gave us the wisdom we needed. He has been called a hero, a champion of freedom and knowledge, and in his poem called "The Litanies of Satan," Charles Baudelaire called him "the familiar healer of human distress." Satanists can echo that statement.

This is a devotional book. It is for beginners and for the devotee who has walked the Satanic path for many years. The prayers are meant to be said at any time of the day or they can be used during a ritual. The hymns can be sung the way you wish to sing them as there is no music included. The chants and affirmations can be used for ritual and meditation. I have written the rituals so that the devotee can perform them on their own. This is because many Satanists don't belong to a local coven but want to be able to perform these kinds of rites.

I invite all devotees of Satan and those who are interested in starting on the path to join me in learning more about this magnificent being whose power and dominion has shaken the cosmos. He has always existed and has been worshipped throughout the earth from the very beginning. He calls his chosen ones to himself and appears in many forms including the Serpent, Raven, Dragon, Goat, and Peacock. With his resounding voice, he has manifested his reality into this world. He is the Devil who has been ridiculed for centuries but his time has arrived. He has come forth to greet those he has called. No longer will his enemies speak for him.

It is my hope that this book will help the devotee of Satan to strengthen their connection to the Prince of Darkness. That by praying the prayers and performing the rituals, you will have a deeper understanding of who Satan is and how you can interact with him. Listen for his voice and allow him to speak to you. Allow the affirmations to descend into your subconscious, and then say them in truth and with confidence.

I thank Satan for his presence in my life and for being my muse in writing this book. I am honoured that he has called me, and that I was able to serve him in this way. Everything I have written here has been done as a form of worship and devotion, and it comes from the heart with a deep love for Satan. He has been here for me in the good and the bad and he is my everything. May he bless this book and guide those who read it.

Are you ready to receive his covenant?

Satanic Blessings,
Marie RavenSoul

PRAYERS TO SATAN

VOW OF ALLEGIANCE

Lord Satan,
Horned One of the Sabbath.
I come before you,
alone.
My soul exposed.
In complete devotion,
I kneel.
Receive this from me,
my greatest desire.
You are my Master,
and I am your Chosen.

Beautiful and majestic,
you emanate such amazing strength.
My eyes are fixed upon you in admiration.
Darkness surrounds you,
a cloak befitting for my King.
I know who you truly are,
the Primordial One.
I embrace your total essence.
My Satan.
My Lucifer.

I dedicate myself to you,
in this life and the next.
No matter what the cost,
I will carry out your Will.
I fight by your side in battle.
Your enemies are my enemies,
your cause is my cause.
Never will I betray you.
Delight or pain,
I will follow you anywhere.

I pledge my allegiance to you.
Before all the Demons,
my eternal witnesses.
Before the gods and goddesses of old,
who stand in quiet acknowledgment.
Before the angels of light,
who dare not raise a hand against me.
Before Jehovah and his Christ,
who must admit defeat.
Before nature,
as it celebrates in song.
Before the world,
its arguments now silenced.

I renew the oaths I made to you long ago;
the ones written with care,
and those expressed in thought alone.
I wear your symbols with pride and love,
an outward statement that I am yours.
Use the words I speak to serve your purpose,
and may my identity be a testimonial to you.
And when it is time for me to take my last breath,
I shall be staring into your dark eyes.
I choose with my entire being,
to spend eternity with you.
So be it.
Nema!

PRAYER OF INVOCATION

Lord Satan...
You are the Horned One of Old.
The one with whom the witches in ecstasy danced.
You are the Guardian of the Crossroads,
with whom many deals are made.
You are the Gatekeeper,
possessing the secrets of magick.
Come, Lord Satan. Come!

Mighty Lucifer...
You are the Primordial One,
the source of all things.
You are the Serpent,
who sat in wait to give humankind a conscience.
You are the Great Dragon,
the one who will restore the cosmos to its proper state.
Come, mighty Lucifer. Come!

Great Iblis...
You are the Fire,
the traveller of all worlds.
You are the Diviner,
knowing the past, present, and the future which is to come.
You are Creator and Destroyer,
the maintainer of all that is.
Come, Great Iblis. Come!

IN ADORATION

My beloved Satan.
I call you this night.
Come!
So that we may commune together.
Join me at your altar.
The one I have prepared for you.

I seek nothing but your presence,
as you are my God and I adore you.
I humbly offer myself to you.
I dedicate my life to your service.
Use me as you see fit.
It is the way it was meant to be.

I am here,
your willing vessel.
I am here,
your willing messenger.
I am here,
your willing priestess.

I bow before you,
and wait on your word.
Anoint me,
and call me to yourself.
I love you, Lord Satan.
Now and always.
Nema!

THE CALLING

Lord Satan . . .
It is the greatest honour,
to be called by you.
That you chose me out of the multitudes
who live on this planet,
is beyond my comprehension.
What was it that you saw in me?
Am I walking the path that you chose for me in a past life?
Is this a continuation of that journey?
I am grateful.

You were always with me,
overseeing my childhood.
Making sure everything was in just the right place.
That it was just the right time,
for you to reveal yourself to me.
To make your intentions known.
You needed to show me that I was yours,
and that my destiny was secure and in your hands.
O Satan, I am in awe of you.

You placed your signs where I would see them.
Played your magical tunes so I could hear their sweet melody.
Appeared to me in the image you knew
I would accept and not be afraid.
You touched my heart with your essence,
and sent your energy up my spine and through my veins.
Burned your unholy mark upon my soul,
and strategically placed the third eye on
my forehead so I could see you.
Above all, you gave me your Black Flame.
Lord Satan, I love you.
Nema!

SATAN, HORNED ONE . . . YOU ARE!

O Lord Satan, Horned One.
Known to many as Pan.
You are the goat-footed one of old.
Roaming to and fro across the meadows,
and jumping high throughout the forests.
Climbing mountains and at the top declaring,
"I am God."

You speak to us in symbols,
and through images long forgotten,
when myths are read and stories told,
hymns sung on ancient ground,
poetry recited from the mouth of a child.
If we listen closely, we can hear you whisper,
"It is I, Pan!"

Let us dance together in the moonlight,
to your rustic tunes heard throughout the land.
Then as I sleep send me dark dreams,
where we can commune once more.
May your name be spoken with dignity,
until the age that has no end.
You are God! You are Satan! You are Pan!
Nema!

PRAYER BEFORE SLEEP

At the end of this day, Lord Satan,
I thank you.
I thank you.
I thank you.
You are the One, the only One.
The true God of this world,
and of the cosmos itself.
I praise your name, Infernal Majesty.

Thank you,
for everything you have taught me today.
Especially for the lessons that were uncomfortable.
As they forced me to face my fears,
and to come to terms with the issues in which I struggle.
I appreciate the difficult tasks that came before me.
They made me stretch myself,
and allowed me to see what I am made of.

Lord Satan,
I thank you for each gift that you have bestowed upon me.
For instructing me in the ways of the ancients,
and for the people you have taught me through.
For the pleasures in which I have partaken,
and for the experiences that have made me stronger.
Your fire burns within,
as you transform me to be your vessel.

You are the mighty Prince of Darkness.
The raven of the night.
I ask if I may enter your dark realm as I sleep,
so that I may be in your unholy presence.
Guide me unto yourself, Satan,
and may I be forever grasped in your mighty wings.
I love you.
All glory be unto you.
Nema!

LUCIFER, LORD OF LIGHT

O Lucifer, Lord of Light.
Radiant One, Morning Star.
Your light shines in the darkness,
revealing the truth of your kingdom.
What was once hidden,
is now being shown to your chosen ones.

May we keep silent,
guarding your secrets entrusted to us.
We will serve you with complete loyalty.
Promising to obey you always.
Our work is to do what you ask of us,
for the furtherance of your kingdom.

You have revealed yourself to those you deem worthy.
May we carry your light forth to where you send us.
This world is yours,
but many do not know of your true nature.
As you have willed it so,
you have cloaked yourself in darkness.

O Lucifer, O Lucifer.
Your glory shines forever.
May your name be spoken with reverence,
through the lips of every man and woman.
We are here.
Waiting for your next move.
Nema!

SATAN, I AM YOURS

Conqueror of the assailant of knowledge,
you changed the universe forever.
Your foot rests on Jehovah's back in endless victory.
Applause echoes throughout the cosmos,
an eternal celebration.
On the highest mountain,
you reveal your glory to those you choose.
Yet in the eyes of the masses,
you are veiled in darkness.
O Satan,
I am yours.

Ancient Serpent,
you called me before my birth.
My soul responded in sudden rapture.
I could not resist you.
Your presence alone demonstrates illimitable authority,
an unquenchable fire that brought me to your side.
O Satan,
I am yours.

Mournful One,
you weep for many things unseen.
Your burdens,
I could only wish to understand.
Might I carry even one to ease your pain,
but this, you would never permit.
For you would not have me endure something which is not
mine.
O Satan,
I am yours.

Master of Magick,
you walk with crystal ball concealed.
Holding secrets many would give their very soul to have.
But for too long,
people have abused your gifts.
Using them,
and attributing them to entities not worthy.
An awful surprise is in store for them,
and one day they will admit their folly.
O Satan,
I am yours.

Muse of Creativity,
you make it possible for humanity to express itself.
Having freed minds from the grip of a false god.
Throughout time,
you have guided the hand of many creators.
Manifesting works that have influenced many cultures and
individuals.
You have reached where no one else has been able to,
my soul.
O Satan,
I am yours.
Hail Satan!

PRAYER TO EXPOSE THE ABRAHAMIC RELIGIONS

Lord Satan, Ancient One.
Reveal to the world,
the true nature of the God of Abraham, Isaac, and Jacob.
For thousands of years, his followers have called you the evil
one.
Yet Jehovah has killed millions of innocents,
including children and animals in his brutal sacrifices.
As the Accuser,
expose him and all his evil actions.

Lord Satan...
Since birth, many have been programmed to believe the Bible.
They live as slaves to a god they only know through words.
This book has caused many to live in fear of eternal
punishment.
They feel shame because they have been taught that they are
'sinners.'
If they would only realize that the greatest deception is the
concept of 'sin.'
Used by the tyrant god to control humanity.
Show them reality and set the world free.

Please help your chosen ones.
Many struggle with having been brainwashed by clergy.
Take the Bible from their hands and minds.
Destroy it!
Set hymns and catechism ablaze,
and make communion wafers crumble to dust.
Expose the traditions of old as empty promises.
In exchange, give them the truth of what was, is now, and that
which is to come.
Nema!

SORROWFUL YEARNING

Lord Satan-Lucifer...
I adore you.
You unveiled yourself to me long ago,
and I am mesmerized by your beauty.
As I look to the horizon,
I ponder your magnificence.
You are the king of the world,
and you have chosen me as your prophet.
I believe in you.
I trust in you.

Thinking of you,
tears run down my face.
I long to be where you are.
Your infernal kingdom is my true home.
By the river, you tell stories to the little ones.
I listen attentively to your words of wisdom.
"Behold," you proclaim. "I am the Master."
Yes, and I will follow you always.
If you were to call me to yourself I would come,
but I must first complete the tasks that you have assigned to
me.

You have forced your enemies to be silent.
Ripped their tongues from their mouths and clamped their
lips shut.
Standing upon the highest precipice,
your glory is revealed to the cosmos.
Who dares to compel you?
Your laughter renders them useless with their mere attempt.
Their destruction is near.
I bow before you in reverence.
You have taken my heart and set it on fire.
Satan-Lucifer, I love you.
Nema!

BESTOW UPON ME, SATAN

Bestow upon me, Satan,
the characteristics of the Dragon.
Overwhelming strength,
vanquishing all weakness.
Uncompromising power,
to manifest my Will.
A fierce presence,
in the face of my enemies.
Dreadfully protective,
a shield for those I care about.
May its fire burn in my spirit,
keeping the black flame bright.

Bestow upon me, Satan,
the characteristics of the Serpent.
Possessing ancient wisdom,
creative in my solitude.
Believably cunning,
so I can make my way in life.
Extremely ruthless,
for when people attack.
In constant renewal,
rising each day ready to do your work.
May its venom run through my soul,
till it consumes me.

Bestow upon me, Satan,
the characteristics of the Peacock.
Prideful in appearance,
always showing off my beauty.
Immortal spirit,
living on throughout the ages.
Steadfast in everything,
willing to go anywhere necessary.

Regal in stature,
a presence to be reckoned with.
May its essence fill my body,
making every step one of confidence.

Bestow upon me, Satan,
the characteristics of the Raven.
Forever watchful,
never ceasing to observe those around me.
Highly intelligent,
knowing what to do in every situation.
A spiritual figure,
so I can teach others about you.
Master of death,
embracing it when my time has come.
May its darkness surround me,
where every living being will feel you with me.

Bestow upon me, Satan,
the characteristics of the Goat.
Stubborn in the face of adversary,
never thwarted in my goals.
Courageous without limits,
climbing every mountain in my way.
Enduring in the advent of fear,
doing what others dare not.
Wild to the point of abandon,
free to live my life the way I see fit.
May its energy ignite my faith and desire,
forever holding high the horns of Baphomet.
Nema!

IN SATAN'S SERVICE

I am forever your servant.
Shrouded in darkness eternally,
I wear your symbols to keep you close.
No one in this world or the next can change that, Lord Satan.

Opposition afflicts me as I grow closer to my goals.
Our enemy does not accept defeat.
You have taught me magick to protect myself,
and you have never taken your presence from me.

You are the source of all that is me.
Your essence runs through me like blood.
Each breath I take I fill myself with your energy.
It is my light and my dark.

As a waterfall is to a stream,
pouring in strength and power,
giving it life and meaning.
This is what you are to me.

Change is coming and as I prepare,
let me do your Will, Lord Satan.
I have given you my body as a vessel,
my mouth for you to speak.

May my life be an act of devotion.
A sacrifice for the ancient one.
I want my work for you to make a difference,
and be the cause of much unrest.

Satan, possess my mind, my body, and my soul.
Make me more like you.
As it was in past times, so will it be in the future.
Great and fierce Serpent, I wait on your word.
Nema!

MY MASTER

Master Satan . . .

You have opened the door,
so I can begin a new life.
Through your wisdom, I begin a new path.
The crossroads are behind me.

There is no escaping your power.
You consume me till only your presence remains.
Energy rises through my spine till it reaches my mind.
I shake in ecstasy as you touch my spirit.

Satan, you reached out your hand,
offered me your chalice to drink.
How could I have said no?
You have placed your mark upon me.

I drink your elixir,
and I offer you, my soul.
I am forever bonded to you, my Master.
I will be obedient to you always.

I wear the ring you have given me.
I am yours.
Never will I belong to another.
My devotion is eternal.

I will follow you everywhere.
Till death, I will fight for your cause.
You hold my life in your hands,
till you call me home.
Nema!

TESTIMONY OF THE SATANIC WARRIOR

Majestic Satan . . .
You give us the power to trample the remnants
of Christianity that are left in this world.
Fill us with your essence,
and let it run through our veins, our souls,
our minds, and our entire being.

We trample on the cross.
We spit upon the book of lies.
We desecrate the virgin whore.
Forever standing proud against the Abrahamic god,
we blaspheme his holy spirit and laugh at his suffering.

We inspire those in shackles to break free
from his tyrant ways.
Enticing them to take that precious bite,
so they will be delivered for evermore.
You are the mighty one, Lord Satan,
and you have bestowed upon us the knowledge
that has made us what we are today.

We hail your name,
and stand strong with you for all eternity.
You inspire us to complete the work you have for us.
We are warriors for you in this world and beyond,
standing up to our enemies and yours alike.
We honour you through our words, our actions,
and our thoughts.
Each day that we live upon this earth,
may we grow stronger in our love for you.

You are our Father, our Teacher, our Muse, our Everything,
and we have taken your mark in dedication.
The universe will know that we are yours.
So place your mighty hand upon us,
and lead us further down your infernal path.
Hail Satan!

PRAYER UPON WAKING

Hail Lucifer!
At the start of this new day,
I call out to you and I know that you hear me.
You are the Light Bringer,
Son of the Morning.
Illuminate this world,
as you rise upon the mountains.
This day is yours.

Give me the strength to walk your path without hesitation,
so that I can make a difference for you wherever I go.
Lead me to places where I will gain wisdom,
and to sources where I will receive knowledge.
Push me to strengthen my abilities,
so that no minute will be lost to laziness, inactivity, or
boredom.
Use the experiences that I will have today,
to teach me more of your ways.

I ask if you may open new doors for me,
so that I can better myself in all areas of my life.
Watch over me this day,
and protect me from my enemies.
Wherever I am,
may people see you within me.
In everything I do,
may you be honoured.
Nema!

SATAN'S TEMPLE

Black candles I light in your honour,
Lord Satan.
I invoke you this precious moment.
Your sigil I have drawn.
I cut my flesh.
I give you, Satan,
my life force.
My blood is spilled for your victory.

Come into me as I open myself.
Your essence consumes my soul.
I am yours,
forever and eternally.
How could I love anyone more than you?
It is not possible.
I live for you.

My body is yours to make your Will manifest.
My mind is given to you,
to create what you desire us to know.
My spirit declares your glory everywhere I travel.
My soul is my ultimate sacrifice to you,
my Master.

Satan,
you fill my mind and transform me.
Darkness overcomes me,
and I bask in its infernal pleasures.
Your presence surrounds me,
therefore, I am never alone.
With bended knee before your altar,
I have made eternal oaths that can never be broken.
May you be glorified in everything I do.

Foundations have been shifted as you work in my life.
Where once there was light—there is darkness.
Where there was stagnation—now there is chaos.
Where once there was love—there is hatred.
Where there was weakness—now there is strength.

Satan,
I am your temple.
I feel your presence increasing within me.
When people look at me,
they see you.
As they feel me,
they feel you.
I anoint them with my blood.
When they drink of me,
they drink of you.

I praise you eternally,
Lord Satan.
Prince of Darkness...
Ancient Serpent...
You are great and majestic,
with a beauty that shines more than the sun.
You are wise and beyond all understanding,
and darker than the deepest chasm in the universe.
I embrace your darkness.
I embrace your light.
With you,
I have all I need.
Ave Satanas!

AM I CALLED?

Satan . . .
I look upon your pentagram,
and I am reminded of when my eyes first settled upon its
regal shape.
Its energy penetrated my mind,
and reached down into my soul, making it unholy.

Have you called me, Satan?

Your path is not an easy one.
It consumes and devours.
There is nothing like it, so overwhelming.
I ask you to come,
reveal to me your power.

Do I have what it takes to follow you, Satan?

How I long to join your Sabbath.
To dance without oppression and to revel in ecstasy.
I must be here for a reason,
calling out your name in anticipation.
You are the eternal God.

Can you teach me your ways, Satan?
Nema!

PRAYER FOR ENDURANCE AND HEALING

Wonderful Satan, bearer of pain.
You above all know what it is like to hurt.
To suffer alone in the darkness,
as well as in the light.
No place is free from pain,
it touches all.
Your anguish is greater than anyone could ever endure.
It is not of the flesh, mind, or spirit,
but of your very essence.
You scream where no ears can hear,
expressing all that is inside.
Making the mountains tremble.

I ask that you come to me as I suffer.
My spirit is ripping apart,
and my body cripples me to nothing.
I am alone,
and no one can take this from me.
I must endure,
or be eaten away by what ails me.
You are the only one who knows what I go through,
and it is you that I approach.
You are the example of perfect strength.
As I think of you,
I know that I can face anything.

Lord Satan,
I invoke you within me.
In this time of trouble,
I ask if you can relieve me of this unbearable pain.
I feel as if I can no longer go on.
I am tired, so tired.
May you fill my body and mind with your essence.

I need to be empowered not from without,
but from within.
So, I can live my life to the fullest.
To be a fighter till the end.
A victor amid the calamities in the world.
Nema!

THANK YOU, SATAN

Satan!
For all the things you mean to me,
I thank you.
For the joy in my heart, the life in my spirit,
I give you thanks.
Satan . . .
My Father . . .
You give me a reason to live.

You give my life meaning.
Every day is a treasure in which you encourage me to grow.
You nudge me to enjoy every minute.
The signs you give me,
I treasure.
The dreams you send,
they guide me.
Your presence reassures me I am not alone.
And for that,
there are no words.
Energy you give me when I am weak.
Strength you pour into my being,
when I must walk the difficult walk.

When I am sad,
you comfort me.
When people hurt me,
you let me know that you are on my side.
You are everything I will ever need.

You're my Father,
who I go to with everything.
My Teacher,
who guides me in all knowledge.

My Protector,
when I am in danger.
My Creator,
who made me who I am.
Above all, Satan,
you are my God with whom I will spend eternity.

Thank you,
with all my heart.
Thank you,
from the depths of my spirit.
Thank you,
with all that I am.
Nema!

APPEAL FOR GUIDANCE

Teach me, Lord Satan,
the knowledge of the ages.
Guide me in thy wisdom,
and let me feel thy presence.

Manifest to me as you will.
Don't let me be bound by irrefutable doctrines,
but lead me to true freedom.
Give me the strength to leave my comfort zone,
and to explore what is forbidden by those who believe they
are wise.

Take away the fear that binds me,
and set me on my true path.
Yet if you don't think I am ready,
let it be as a sunrise.
Allow me to see your light as well as your darkness,
the fullness of who you are.

Satan!
Great Dragon!
Lucifer!
Prince of Darkness!

If I could have anything,
it would be to know your truth.
To believe in what is real,
and not in the insanity of others.
So, as I walk down this narrow road,
don't let me be discouraged.
As it was you who placed me upon it.
Nema!

PRAYER OF DEVOTION

Lord Satan,
I feel your infernal presence surrounding me.
You are the Great Serpent,
who gives me knowledge and wisdom.
The Great Dragon,
who will lead me into the coming battle.
I desire to serve you with my entire mind, body, soul, and
spirit.
I open myself up to you today, tomorrow, and forever.
Eternally, I will walk by your side.

Lord Satan,
you are my Master, Teacher, God, and Father.
I adore you with my innermost being.
My mind is filled with thoughts of you.
Your essence fills my spirit and your energy runs through my
veins.
I long to hear your words.
To know your greatest mysteries.
When you call to me, I will come.
By the water, I will find you.

Lord Satan,
you are the most powerful of all.
I bow before your magnificence.
Receive my offering.
I invoke you, Ancient One.
Rise, rise in power.
May the world be witness to your glory.
Live through me and manifest your Will.
I love you.
Nema!

SATAN, MY MASTER

As the incense rises into the air,
I call upon your name, Lord Satan.
The shadow who roams the earth,
your essence is felt in every nation.
You have been known by many names,
and there is not a place in this world that you have not
manipulated.

To the ancient Egyptians,
you were Set.
To the Persians,
you were Ahriman.
To the Greeks,
you were Pan.

Master of the carnival,
you slither throughout the midway rides.
Master of the fair,
you hover over the magician's hand.
Master of the festival,
you caress the musicians as they play their song.

Your darkness consumes my spirit.
Your light transforms my mind.
I cannot resist you,
nor would I ever try.
Possess me, make me yours.
O Lord Satan, my Master.
You are the One.
Nema!

A DECLARATION

Satan,
you are beyond compare.
Fathomless wisdom,
deeper than all others.
Your power exceeds that of all gods,
and your presence alone commands respect.
The Prince of Darkness,
you have been named.
God of this World!

Secure in who you are,
your confidence overcomes all insults and injury.
You have much to share,
much to teach,
to all who trust in you.
Among many,
you choose a few.
You guide us along the way,
without a book,
not through those who pretend they know you more.

You are often silent,
but give words and signs when they are needed.
And often when they are not,
but just because.
You say, "No more" when we begin to kneel,
but instead "Rise, stand strong."
We call you Father, Friend, and Lord.
But above all,
you are our God.
Nema!

PAN, GOD OF PROPHECY, COME!

Guardian of the ancient temples,
you keep watch with glaring eye.
With a stomp of your hooves,
wolves, hares, and deer stand at attention—waiting.
You rule the forest under the sun,
prancing through healing waters.
And under the moon,
giving refuge in hidden caves.

From Arcadia to Rome, and throughout the earth,
you have revealed yourself, horns high.
Your priests and priestesses kneel at your altar,
singing ancient hymns in your honour.
O Pan, O Pan, play your pipes,
so your worshippers can dance all through the night.
It is said that you are the god of prophecy.
Do you have a fortune to bestow upon me?

Crowned with a wreath of pine, O King,
you are the hunter, shepherd, and friend.
Come! Come, Goat-God.
Giver of many gifts.
Yet only one do I request,
that is to prophesy at your behest.
I love you, Pan, Satan, Devil.
Memorized by your sacred tune,
I will follow you forever.
So, mote it be!

MY BELOVED

Beloved Satan . . .
I need your presence in my life,
just as one needs air to breathe.
To be without you,
would be to die.

Your love is like no other love.
It is overwhelming,
most powerful and complete.
It reaches to the depths of my soul.
Showing me that what I thought was love,
was not love at all.

You teach me day after day,
night after night.
I am insatiable for your untold wisdom.
You have shown me ancient things,
which I will cherish for eternity.

If home is where the heart is,
my home is with you.
As it was and will always be.
Nema!

FROM SEA TO SEA

Lord Satan . . .
Among the ashes, you have risen.
Across the desert, you roam.
Upon the mountain tops, you are exalted.
Your devotees sing in celebration,
and dance at the sound of your name.

Satan, I listen for your voice.
Satan, I wait for your presence.
Satan, I long to hear your call.

You have come for the sake of adversity.
Never allowing the world to become complacent,
you have struck chaos into the heart of humanity.
As the sun rises in the east,
you tear the veil between the living and the dead.
The cosmos trembles at your magick.

Satan, I listen for your voice.
Satan, I wait for your presence.
Satan, I long to hear your call.

From sea to sea,
your warriors gather.
At your battle cry, they go forth.
The war will end in your victory.
A change is coming that you have set in motion.
The eyes of humanity will be opened for evermore.

Satan, I listen for your voice.
Satan, I wait for your presence.
Satan, I long to hear your call.
Nema!

EXPRESSION OF GRATITUDE

Amazing Satan!
Thank you,
for everything you have done for me.
From the time I can remember,
you have been by my side.
Inciting me when I have fallen.
Yet never do you pick me up,
knowing I am capable of that on my own.
You believed in me when no one else did—
not even myself.
Watching over me through the good and the bad,
you held back your hand when I went through hardship.
As I had to become stronger and wiser.
For that,
I give you the greatest respect.

Thank you,
for the times you allowed me to tread on a different path.
Even though it wasn't yours.
You wanted me to learn the ways of the enemy,
so in the face of conflict, I would have the upper hand.
I did learn,
and my hatred for the false god grew.
It is my Will to share my knowledge with others.
I am honoured,
that you have given me the desire to help those who struggle,
those who hear your call,
but Christian programming holds them back.
May you give them the strength to break free—
and stay free.

Thank you,
for always wanting the best for me.
Preparing me to wield a sword if need be.

For putting up with my inability to push on at times,
and for my laziness and lack of devotion.
For the secret knowledge you impart to me at your altar,
making me evolve as a person and as a Satanist.
You have been my muse since I was a child,
motivating me to create and change the world.
My feelings can never be expressed through mere words,
so I offer you everything I have to give, my Lord Satan.
I love you.
Nema!

ALL I HAVE

Your presence surrounds me,
like fog over a lake on a summer morn.
Your black flame bestowed upon me,
burns dim, but cannot be extinguished.
No matter where I run,
I cannot escape you.
Wherever I turn,
you are there.

You allowed me to wander,
but all in your timing.
Knowledge had to be taken,
like a jewel from a secret vault.
You enticed me back to your side,
yet twisting and turning, I fought.
But I knew that I must come home,
as that is where I belong.

My mind is filled with memories,
like drawings in an ancient cavern.
Your essence is unlike any other,
darkness and light merged in power.
My soul has always yearned for you.
When I am far,
it is incomplete.
Your call reaches me through space and time,
an impression on my spirit.

Your energy pulses through my veins,
and excitement rises as I begin anew.
For I belong under your precious wings,
where all strength lies.
You are the amazing one,
Lord Satan.

If only I could see you before me,
your beauty and power would keep me in awe.

If I could sing a song—I would lift my voice to the stars to
announce your truth.
If I could play you a sonata—I would hope to make you smile.
If I could dance in worship—I would express to you the love
that fills my heart.
If I could paint an image—I would create a masterpiece
flaunting your magnificence.
But all I have is this prayer—expressed in adoration.
Nema!

IBLIS, RISE!

Iblis! Shaytan!
At such a time as this—Rise!
The world needs your presence.
Reveal yourself.
May your power be seen by all.
Surprise your enemies, bring them low.
Paralyze them, strike fear into their core.

Lord Iblis . . .
Rise over the mountains.
Rise over the sea.
Rise over the desert.
Lord Iblis, you are the true God.

Whisper in the ears of the corrupt politicians.
Thwart their twisted plans.
No longer shall they deceive the world.
Take the power from their hands.
Cause chaos among the religious leaders.
Reveal the falsity of their books.
Start a rebellion, which turns them into dust.

Lord Iblis . . .
Rise over the mountains.
Rise over the sea.
Rise over the desert.
Lord Iblis, you are the true God.

Many seek you in the desert.
See their hearts and hear their call.
Protect them from those who wish them harm.
Be a refuge for them in war.
May they hear your voice,
and know they are not alone.
Lord Iblis, you are here and we give you thanks.
Nema!

REQUEST FOR EMOTIONAL HEALING

When insecurity hits me like a raging wind,
be with me, Father Satan.

When doubt strikes me like lightning,
remind me of truth.

When fear overpowers me,
hold me in your wings, Great Dragon.

If pain grabs me like a claw,
heal me with your mighty power.

When depression fills me like water in a well,
shower my soul with joy, beautiful Peacock Angel.

If anxiety creeps through my mind and takes over my
thoughts,
place me on solid ground.

When I think that I am not good enough,
make my spirit shine as a star, Wise Serpent.

And if I feel that it is too hard to go on,
give me strength.
Nema!

CALL TO ME, SATAN-LUCIFER

Lord Satan . . .
Your influence is greater than that of all the gods.
Up above and down below,
you rule over the darkness and the light is under your
command.
You cannot be denied.
You cannot be contained.

All hail Satan-Lucifer.
Baphomet revealed.
Malevolent.
Benevolent.
Energy intertwined.
Sabbatic Goat supreme.

Call me to your banquet.
Allow me to celebrate with you.
May I be deemed worthy to sit at your table?
Your kingdom reigns,
as it has always reigned.
My King.

Demonic wings unfurled.
Displaying your infernal majesty.
You are the lightning that struck the Earth,
making it subservient to your Will.
I worship you.
Rise, Satan-Lucifer! Rise.
Nema!

PRAYER FOR SATANIST LEADERS

Lord Satan . . .
Mighty One . . .
Wisdom Incarnate . . .
Speaker of Knowledge . . .
I ask that you bestow your blessings on the leaders of our
Satanic community.
Guide us,
so that we will serve you in the ways that you desire.
Give us strength,
to keep going when things get tough.
Bestow upon us wisdom,
so we will know what to do in all situations.
Inspire us to encourage one another,
instead of tearing each other down.
So we will use our words to bless instead of curse.
Yet push us to stand tall when we face things that are wrong.
To fight if we have to,
yet strive for peace.

Help us, Father,
to be there for your children- both the adept and the new.
To guide them in learning what you have for them.
To encourage them not to follow anyone but you,
and to find their own path.
Let us not forget what it was like when we first came to you.
How you were gentle, kind, and patient.
May we follow in your footsteps.
To love as you love,
and teach as you teach.

We are happy to be your servants,
reveal to us the hidden things.
Try us,
so we may be worthy of your affairs
that you place in our hands.

Bestow on us your covenant as we trust in you.
Let us receive your counsel,
not acting unless it is your Will.
It is an honour to serve you, Lord Satan.
Thank you for choosing us.
May our lives be devoted to you,
and may we be a reflection of who you are to the world.
Watch over us,
and bless your people.
Lord Satan,
may it be done according to your Will.
Nema!

FATHER'S DAY

On this Father's Day,
I honour you, my Father Satan.
I thank you for being in my life,
guiding, teaching, comforting, and loving me.
You were with me when I was a child.
As I grew,
you revealed yourself.
I will never forget that day,
when I first saw your precious name on the stone.
When everyone else was scared,
I looked in awe.
Then when I felt your power in the cloud,
I could not drag my eyes away.

You waited till I was old enough to lead me to believe in you,
and to follow in your footsteps.
Then you guided me throughout the toughest years in life,
showing me I was your child.
Your strength gave me the courage to keep striving.
Your Will made me go on.
When I was alone,
you were there.
That meant everything to me.
You taught me about you,
so I would understand.

Yet I left you behind,
and you let me go so I could experience and learn new things.
When it was time to come back,
you called me.
I have put you through some tough times,
I am sure.
But like the father you are,

you have always been there.
Remaining in the shadows as I did my own thing.
Then coming to my side when I needed your help, protection,
and guidance.

There is no one like you.
You are the Amazing One.
The Morning Star who brings to light a new day.
Who cares to show his child what he has done in the early
morning,
by waking me up.
You are full of surprises.
You are known by many names-
Satan, Lucifer, Melek Ta'us, Blue God.
But on this day,
I honour you as Father.
Nema!

DESCEND, O SERPENTINE

O Great Serpent, come to me.
Come this night on flying wings.
This night of nights,
I offer myself,
to you.
To you, my great serpentine Lord.

Come slither into my dreams.
Take over my mind,
and bring me to new heights.
Consume the energy that I give to you.
May you be satisfied with my offering.
Take, take it from me.

I open my mouth to receive you.
As I take a deep breath,
I feel you enter.
Welcome.
Welcome.
Let us dance together.

Descend within me, Serpentine.
Consume and devour.
Your venom runs through my veins,
and your power rises as I surrender.
Possess me fully.
My body is yours.
Nema!

SATAN, WHO YOU ARE TO ME

Lord Satan,
you give me the energy that flows through my veins.
And the joy that floods my heart.
Wisdom given when the time is right,
an impression on my soul.
Sweet words in a whisper...

My heart is racing,
full of emotion.
A love once given,
is now given back.
A blanket of comfort over my being,
a peace that transcends all.
Words unspoken,
but thought.
Feelings beyond a poet's mind.
Quiet contemplation of who you are.
One beyond description...

You are in the clouds that sail across the sky.
In the wind,
crashing waves against the shore.
In the sound of rustling leaves,
and in the beauty of a waterfall.
You are the power of a volcano,
and the chaos of an earthquake.
You can be found in the vastness of the night,
and in the dawn of a new day.
Creator and Destroyer...

As I walk, you are beside me,
and when I sleep, you give me dreams.
When I cry,

you place your wings over me for comfort.
You remind me of who I am.
When I need someone to talk to,
you send a friend.
When I sing you a song,
you listen.
When I am sad,
you take away the pain.
When I forget certain treasures,
you remind me.
I went away,
and you let me go to learn.
When it was time,
you brought me home.
Nema!

ACKNOWLEDGMENT OF SATAN'S DOMINION

Precious Satan . . .
As I light this candle on your altar,
I raise my hands in devotion.
Your presence in this darkness,
is clothed with ancient wisdom.
Your great strength envelops me.
Satan, you are my Teacher.

Precious Satan . . .
Your reality is known throughout the world.
Only fools deny your existence.
Expose the false ones.
And when it is time,
their deceit will be known to all.
Satan, you are my God.

Precious Satan . . .
I want to live my life for you.
Thank you for choosing me as one of your own.
I know that you have your eye on me.
May I pass the tests you give,
and may I serve you well.
Satan, you are my Master.
Nema!

CHANTS OF DEVOTION

Lord Satan, supreme ruler.
Power and dominion are yours. Test me!
And may I be found worthy in your sight.
Lord Satan, supreme ruler.

***

Hail! Hail! Hail Lucifer!
Light Bringer.
Herald of the dawn.
Illuminate the desolate ones.
Hail! Hail Lucifer!

***

Hail the Horned One!
Ruler of the forest. God of the earth.
Come! Come, and join me at your sacred fire.
Hail the Horned One!

***

Melek Ta'us! Peacock Angel!
Your beauty is beyond compare.
If it is your Will,
show me the hidden things.
Melek Ta'us! Peacock Angel!

***

Shaitanic fire, rise. Rise!
Move within the world.
Appear to your chosen ones.
We are ready.
Shaitanic fire, rise. Rise!

***

Hail! Hail! Hail Satan!
Cunning Serpent, embodiment of forbidden knowledge.
Slither into my eager mouth and descend.
Descend into the depths of me.
Transform me in accordance with your Will.
Hail Satan! Satan! Satan!

Melek Ta'us! Satan
You have always existed,
and shall have no end.
I trust you.
I am ready to receive your covenant.
Melek Ta'us! Satan!

***

Hail Satan! Great Dragon!
Purify and purge.
You are needed here.
Hail Satan! Great Dragon!

***

God of the Witches, I honour you.
You have been worshiped throughout the earth.
Your followers loyal unto death.
God of the Witches, I honour you.

***

Lord Satan! Lord Satan!
Prince of Darkness. Ruler of the Abyss.
Come. Come. Come this night.
Consume me. Devour me.
Lord Satan, come!

***

O Devil! Come! Come forth!
Carnal beast, ferocious spirit.
Come forth. Let your power reign.
O Devil! Come! Come forth!

***

Lord Lucifer! Wise one.
May your knowledge be revealed to your chosen.
Ancient and majestic you are.
Lord Lucifer! Wise one.

Ancient Serpent, return!
Slither throughout the earth. Disrupt!
Bring it under your command.
Ancient Serpent, return!

***

O Devil! Great Accuser.
Ridiculed for centuries.
Your time has come.
Come forth!
Greet your child.
O Devil! Great Accuser.

***

Io Pan! Io Pan! Io Pan!
God of strength. God of fertility.
Climb the mountains high.
Dance along the luscious streams.
I will follow you everywhere.
Io Pan! Io Pan! Io Pan!

***

Lucifer! Power of the air.
King! Beautiful king. Appear in your brilliance.
Lucifer! Power of the air.

***

Dragon of primordial fire.
Rise! Rise! Rise!
At the mention of your name, Lord Satan,
people shall tremble once again.
Dragon of primordial fire.

***

Blue God, magnificent king.
All glory belongs to you.
I honour your symbol and your image,
for they remind me of you.
Blue God, magnificent king.

Horned One! Lord of the Dance!
Lead your children to sing.
To dance with joy before you.
Horned One! Lord of the Dance!

***

O Lucifer! Bright Morning Star!
Let your light shine upon me.
Stand upon the highest mountain.
Reveal your glory.
O Lucifer! Bright Morning Star!

***

Ancient Serpent, rise.
Rise!
Ascend and appear.
Ancient Serpent, rise.

***

Satan, teacher of ancient secrets.
You lead without a book.
Your chosen ones hear your voice.
I seek your wonders and receive your miracles.
Satan, teacher of ancient secrets.

***

Lord Satan! Dragon of chaos.
Change this world.
Make it quake.
The old order shall pass away.
Lord Satan! Dragon of chaos.

***

Lord Satan, purifying fire.
Awaken me from dormancy.
I will serve you eternally.
Lord Satan, purifying fire.

Satan! Primordial Serpent.
Encircle the Earth.
Terrify!
Your enemies quake in fear.
Satan! Primordial Serpent.

***

Mighty Lucifer, the true light.
Shine! Shine! Shine!
Brilliant one. Most powerful.
Mighty Lucifer, the true light.

***

Lord Satan, mystical raven.
Come forth from the darkness.
Fly through my dreams.
Lord Satan, mystical raven.

***

O Devil, enemy of the Christian god.
Reveal yourself to the world.
No longer shall your enemies speak for you.
Voice the truth!
O Devil, enemy of the Christian god.

***

Hail! Hail! Hail Satan!
Your treasures are hidden,
and you bestow them to your faithful.
I will keep your secrets,
and wait for the fulfillment of your promises.
Hail! Hail! Hail Satan!

***

Rise, Satan. Rise!
Set me on the path to freedom.
I will serve you forever.
Rise, Satan. Rise!

O Lucifer, teacher of forbidden knowledge.
Spread your wings. Fly upon the high places.
The aether is under your command.
O Lucifer, teacher of forbidden knowledge.

***

Lord Shaitan! God of fire.
Reign in power. Reign in power.
Throughout the ages, you have been silent.
Your hour has arrived.
Speak! Your voice will be heard.
Lord Shaitan! God of fire.

***

Raven of old.
Majestic in appearance.
You are honoured here, Satan.
Raven of old.

***

Goat God of the wilderness.
Cernunnos! Cernunnos! Cernunnos!
Surrounded by animals big and small,
you are the Lord of the Wild.
The healer of many.
Goat God of the wilderness.

***

Hail to the Devil! Hail!
You are the victor, and sit upon the highest throne.
Hail to the Devil! Hail!

***

Satan! My Lord! My God!
I reject the Abrahamic teachings,
and I will follow you forever.
I will suffer for your sake,
if I am called upon to do so.
Satan! My Lord! My God!

Satan! Melek Ta'us!
You know truth and falsehood.
I will obey you in everything.
Satan! Melek Ta'us!

***

Sabbatic Goat. God of the forest.
Your call has been heard.
I come to you in reckless abandon.
I am yours.
Sabbatic Goat. God of the forest.

***

Eternal one. Morning Star.
Lucifer! Lucifer! Lucifer!
Your light reaches to the ends of the earth.
In solitude, I will meet you.
Eternal one. Morning Star.

***

Ave! Ave! Ave Satanas!
I love you.
I love you.
I love you.
Ave! Ave! Ave Satanas!

***

Lord Satan, master of magick.
I long to hear your message.
Manifest as the raven,
and bestow upon me your wisdom.
Lord Satan, master of magick.

***

Lord Satan! Dragon of fire.
Creator. Destroyer.
Burn all false doctrine.
Replace it with your truth.
Lord Satan! Dragon of fire.

Lord Satan-Lucifer! Hail!
Darkness and light intertwined.
You encompass all things.
Lord Satan-Lucifer! Hail!

***

Melek Ta'us! Blue God.
May your power be felt throughout the earth.
Show me the ways to your kingdom.
Melek Ta'us! Blue God.

***

Lord Satan! Mighty Horned One.
Bringer of eternal darkness.
I give you my allegiance.
I worship you.
Lord Satan! Mighty Horned One.

***

Lord Satan, wise raven.
Sing! Sing! Sing!
Sing your magical tune.
Lord Satan, wise raven.

***

O Shaitan! Mighty and powerful God.
May your wrath fall upon the Abrahamic tyrant.
Send him to the burning fires.
O Shaitan! Mighty and powerful God.

***

Rege Satanas! Rege Satanas! Rege Satanas!
Master of the worlds.
Keeper of the Black Flame.
Rise in power!
Rege Satanas! Rege Satanas! Rege Satanas!

Wise Raven, gatekeeper of the spiritual realm.
Take me to places unknown.
Teach me your magick.
Wise Raven, gatekeeper of the spiritual realm.

***

Satan! Master.
You appear in many forms.
You give and take away.
You cause happiness and misery.
I will be faithful to you always.
Satan! Master.

***

Lucifer! Bringer of knowledge.
The first and true rebel.
Break all delusions.
Lucifer! Bringer of knowledge.

***

Great and powerful Dragon.
Come! Come forth from the fiery depths.
Devour! Consume!
Great and powerful Dragon!

***

Lord Satan. Pan. Goat of the Witches.
You roam the rustic woodlands at night.
Play sweet melodies on your flute by day.
Come! Come! Come!
Lord Satan. Pan. Goat of the Witches.

***

Satan, my Lord!
Thank you.
Thank you.
Thank you.
I am grateful for all you have done.
Satan, my Lord!

HYMNS

PRINCE OF DARKNESS

In the beginning,
a flame burned in you.
It set you apart.
Never were you in the womb,
of some "All."
You had a conscience,
making them want your fall.

O, Prince of Darkness,
keeper of knowledge.
Prince of Darkness,
the ruler of night.
Prince of Darkness,
teacher of secrets.
Lucifer,
bringer of light.

Stagnation was a disease,
forbidding progress.
You stood alone in your frustration,
wanting to move the universe.
You fought for change,
nothing would be the same.

O, Prince of Darkness,
the one who loves.
Prince of Darkness,
the one who hates.
Prince of Darkness,
the fire that burns.
Melek Ta'us,
peacock so blue.

77

Initiation comes from you,
Leader Supreme.
Gifts abound from your courage,
now we can dream.
When there once was nothing,
now there is plenty.
Life can move on,
we are free.

O, Prince of Darkness,
bringer of chaos.
Prince of Darkness,
example of bravery.
Prince of Darkness,
breaker of chains.
Satan,
adversary to slavery.

INNER BLACK FLAME

I am going to find my inner Black Flame.
I am going to find my inner Black Flame.
Oh, I'm going to find my inner Black Flame.
Yes, I'm going to find my inner Black Flame.

I will gain strength from that inner Black Flame.
I will gain strength from that inner Black Flame.
Oh, I'll gain strength from that inner Black Flame.
Yes, I'll gain strength from that inner Black Flame.

I will grow through my inner Black Flame.
I will grow through my inner Black Flame.
Oh, I will grow through my inner Black Flame.
Yes, I will grow through my inner Black Flame.

I will heed that inner Black Flame.
I will heed that inner Black Flame.
Oh, I will heed that inner Black Flame.
Yes, I will heed that inner Black Flame.

Satan created my inner Black Flame.
Yes, Satan created my inner Black Flame.
And it is going to rise and shine.
As I follow in the footsteps of my God.

HYMN TO THE SABBATIC GOAT

O Sabbatic Goat, Dark Lord of the forest.
At your entrance, sparrows sing their happy chorus.
Trees sway and bow.
Wolves begin to howl.
A celebration has begun,
in honour of the One.

Witches dance around the sacred fire.
Naked, exposed and filled with desire.
Strong and muscular, your phallus erect.
You are the master of all carnal acts.
Lavish me with your passionate lust.
With the kiss of shame, I kneel, I trust.

God of fertility, muse to a myriad of poets.
Throughout the ages, to you, they are forever devoted.
You are the moon, the stars, and the sun.
Your work and influence will never be undone.
Come to me this night, with horns raised high.
My love, oh my love, I cannot deny.

FREEDOM FIGHTER

Brilliant One,
you had the courage to stand up for what was right.
Did you know where you would land,
O, Angel of Light?

You took a chance,
and fought a good fight.
As only you would do.

They say it was pride,
the iniquity of old.
But I say you stood for freedom,
defied Jehovah and broke his control.

He threw you down,
and you crashed upon the earth.
But you stood up tall with wings outstretched,
ready for a new birth.

You made the Earth your dwelling place.
Revealed yourself to the human race.
You urged the woman to question the command,
of the one who would have her submit.

Never would he be allowed to oppress with an iron fist,
as you would oppose his every action.
Scream out at his destruction,
unseen by all.

You came alongside those you would teach,
guiding them into all knowledge.
You would never receive credit for your care.
Despised by the masses from the beginning.

But you stand strong,
never giving up.
You are the giver of freedom, O Lucifer.
You give us the strength to throw the cross down,
and help us walk on without fear.
May your mighty wings enshroud us.

SALVE SATANÁS

Salve Satanás, Salve Satanás.
Salve Satanás, Salve Satanás.
Satanás, Mestre do Caos.

Saluto Satana, Saluto Satana.
Saluto Satana, Saluto Satana.
Satana, Antico Uno.

Bucura-te de Satana, Bucura-te de Satana.
Bucura-te de Satana, Bucura-te de Satana.
Satana, Dumnezeu cu Coarne de Sabat.

Salam Setan, Salam Setan.
Salam Setan, Salam Setan.
Setan, Bijaksana Ular.

Ave Satanas, Ave Satanas.
Ave Satanas, Ave Satanas.
Satanas, Princeps Tenebrarum.

Hail Satan, Hail Satan.
Hail Satan, Hail Satan.
Satan, Most Powerful.

HYMN TO IBLIS

Across the barren desert, you brought desolation.
Your arrival was announced by the song of the raven.
In your hand, you carry a scepter of iron.
Going to war to slay your enemy, the liar.

Terrifying Fire, Nameless One.
Iblis, I am devoted to you.
You are King of the World and shine like the sun.
Iblis, you are honoured in this place.

You have risen in the mountains.
Called your warriors to stand and be counted.
Set the heavens aflame with your tongue.
All power is yours, the battle already won.

Terrifying Fire, Nameless One.
Iblis, I am devoted to you.
You are King of the World and shine like the sun.
Iblis, you are honoured in this place.

You speak through dreams to your chosen few.
Obscure to the masses, the one they never knew.
Beyond all names, you appear as a blazing pillar.
Lord of the Djinn, master of all within the mirror.

Terrifying Fire, Nameless One.
Iblis, I am devoted to you.
You are King of the World and shine like the sun.
Iblis, you are honoured in this place.

AFFIRMATIONS TO SATAN

Satan is my God.
The Ancient Serpent who always was.
I seek after him,
and learn his ways.

***

I honour my commitments to Satan.
I live my life according to his decrees.
I will not stray from what I have promised.

***

I know that Satan is real.
My experiences have shown me the truth of his existence.
Atheists might try to dissuade me from my beliefs.
Their words mean nothing to me.

***

I curse the Abrahamic god and all his names.
A lowly desert god is he.
Impotent and powerless.
I stand against his holy texts.

***

Before I was born, Satan placed the Black Flame within me.
Every day I will nurture this Flame.
My priority is my relationship with Satan.
I will take what I learn from him and put it into practice.

***

To say that one is a Satanist without belief
is an insult to the Master.
I am a traditional Witch.
I worship the Devil and serve at his altar.

I raise high the pentagram,
and wear it around my neck with pride.
Satan's symbols will be forever honoured.
I will remember him always.

***

I have dedicated my life to Satan.
I devote each day to him.
His Will is my Will.
My soul yearns to be in his presence.

***

I reject the Abrahamic god and all his works.
I reject Allah and his Quran.
I reject Jehovah and his Torah.
I reject Jesus and his Gospel.
In Satan's name, they are banished.

***

Satan has shown me signs and wonders.
I am forever grateful.
I sing him songs of devotion.

***

I am a Satanist.
Before my birth, Satan chose me.
It is the greatest honour.
I never want to disappoint him.
I will walk his path always.

***

I have given myself to Satan.
In this life and in the next.
It is an eternal bond that can never be broken.
I love Satan with all my heart.

The Satanic path requires discipline.
I fast from food and drink
as part of my spiritual practice.
My focus is on Satan only.

***

I remember the past with Satan always.
His teachings will never escape my mind.
I remember his ancient words.
I teach those he sends me.

***

I treasure the connection I have with Satan.
I honour his symbol
and his image
every day of my life.

***

I walk the path of Satan.
Despite good or bad.
No adversary can rip me from his grasp.

***

I am a messenger of Satan.
I will guide his chosen ones as he directs.
I live according to his Will.

***

I accept Satan's chalice
and drink his elixir.
I drink from it eagerly.
His essence runs through my veins.
I have transformed into his creation.

Satan is primordial.
He was not created as the Abrahamic religions have taught.
His ancient teachings precede all.
He is the source of all wisdom.
I revere him with my mind, spirit, body, and soul.

***

I chose Satan.
But Satan chose me first.
It is a part of me that can never be destroyed.

***

I will follow Iblis to the ends of the earth.
He walks through the desert,
causing desolation and destruction of his enemies.
He is the One.
The most powerful.

***

I raise the chalice in Satan's honour.
I take part in his Will.
It is who I am.

***

Satan is my God.
I kneel before his altar in worship.
I am his own.
This I will never forget.

***

The Satanic path requires study.
I have made a commitment to pursue knowledge,
to do what it takes to be the Satanist I was meant to be.

Satan cannot be contained.
Triangles and circles cannot restrain him.
Words cannot bind him.
Religious objects cannot compel him.
He laughs at such foolishness.

***

I believe in Satan.
His essence is within me.
My eyes shine with his glory.

***

My pride is in being a Satanist.
I declare myself openly as such.
I will never hide my devotion to Satan.
No matter what it might cost me.

***

That old serpent called the Devil and Satan is my God.
His reign will never end.
Only fools worship his enemy.
His power is unmatchable.

***

I became a Satanist because I heard Satan's call.
It was not because I wanted material success, power, or sex.
I did not make a pact to get something in return.
I am a Satanist because I love Satan and believe in his ways.

***

I practice my Satanic religion every day.
Meditation, prayer, and ritual are what
keeps my focus where it belongs.
They are important aspects of my life,
and allow me to be a vessel and channel for Satan.

I am a child of Satan-Lucifer.
I carry both light and dark within me.
He has bestowed upon me great things.
I will glorify his name always.

**

I am loyal to Satan above all.
Through fire, I will follow him.
Through water, I will follow him.
Through hardship, I will follow him.
No situation could deter me from this path.
I belong to Satan.

**

Satan dislikes the mundane,
and hates time wasted on fleeting things.
I vow to focus on the spiritual.
At his altar, I will pray and spend time with him.

**

As a Satanist, it is important to learn the ways of divination.
I study hard to learn different methods.
I use them to communicate with Satan.
It is all about him.

**

The darkness penetrates my soul.
Satan's essence runs through my veins.
I bow before him.
He is deserving of worship.

**

Satan must be given the utmost respect.
The Prince of Darkness serves no one.
I am honoured that he has chosen me.

SPIRITUAL PRACTICES AND RITUALS

THE SATANIC ALTAR

SETTING up and maintaining a Satanic altar is a spiritual practice. This is where you will spend a lot of time in prayer, ritual, and devotion. It is the focal point of your Satanic worship and is an offering to Satan. Your altar should have its own separate room, but if that is not possible, then it should be placed in a respectful place away from regular activity. The altar and the space in front of it is sacred to the devotee and should be treated as such. Other people should not touch or handle the items on the altar. The devotee might choose to place a curtain or border around it to set it apart from the mundane. If that's not possible, you may cover the altar with a cloth.

The altar should be dedicated to Satan immediately after its initial set up, and all items should be consecrated in his name. The devotee of Satan will invest time, energy, and money into the altar. Only items bought specifically for the altar are used. Altar items don't have to be extremely expensive, but they should be purchased with wisdom and be honouring to Satan. It is very important that the altar is clean. Taking care of the altar is a sacred duty.

The devotee may wish to have one side of the altar devoted to Lucifer, the lighter aspect, and the other to Satan, the darker aspect. The choice is up to the individual. If the devotee is also a practitioner of magic, another altar should be made for this purpose. This can be placed beside the altar to Satan.

When approaching the altar, the devotee should do so in an honouring manner as if Satan himself was in front of them. Bow or stand reverently for a couple of minutes before walking up to it, your eyes focused on the image or statue of Satan. You might want to remove your footwear out of respect. Prepare your spirit for what you will say and experience.

If the devotee wishes to perform a ritual outside or if they want to be able to do their devotions while away from home, a make-shift altar can be used. This can be made from a small box or rock.

What is placed on the altar is up to the devotee, although certain items are required for standard Satanic practice. When shopping for these items, ask for Satan's guidance. If you feel drawn to an item, this may be an indicator that you should purchase it. The items listed below are considered the basics for a permanent Satanic altar.

ALTAR TABLE

The surface used for the altar needs to be flat and one that is not used for anything else. Ideally, it would be a table designated for this purpose alone, but in certain cases such as lack of space, the devotee might use the top of a bookcase or dresser. The bigger the surface the better, so being able to find a surface as big as possible that can fit in your allotted space is ideal.

ALTAR CLOTH

The colour of the altar cloth should be black. This is to honour Satan as the Prince of Darkness. The surface should be free of any designs, but the devotee may wish to draw or sew images on the front or sides as a sign of devotion to Satan. If the devotee wants to incorporate the Lucifer aspect, they may wish to place a small blue cloth horizontally in the middle of the altar or put a blue border around the outer edge of the cloth.

IMAGE/STATUE OF SATAN

The image or statue of Satan should be placed in the centre of the altar, either in the middle or the back. This is the focal point of the altar.

DEVOTIONAL BOOK

The devotee should have a special book that they keep on their altar that contains important writings such as prayers, chants, hymns, and affirmations. This is different from a magical journal or book of spells which should be placed on the magical altar instead. It can be added to as time goes on, so it is important to leave space for developing ideas.

DAGGER/ATHAME

The dagger is an important item and should be chosen with care. It should be purchased strictly for devotional and ritual use and not be used for anything else. The devotee might pray to Satan to ask his guidance when going to purchase a dagger. It is used to draw the pentagram in the air before a ritual, for consecrating items, and for placing on the heart during a dedication or promise rite. It is placed horizontally at the front of the altar. It should never point to the image of Satan as that would be disrespectful.

CHALICE

The Satanic chalice will usually be made of stainless steel, silver, or glass. A devotee may choose one that has a pentagram or Sigil of Baphomet on the side or they may want one without any kind of design. The Satanist should never use gold because of its use in the Catholic Mass. A goblet can also be used.

CANDLES

For the Satanic altar, black candles are the primary colour, but for devotions and rituals to Lucifer, blue can be used as well. Red candles are good for showing love and devotion to Satan. Contrary to popular belief, white candles should not be used because of their association with the white light religions. It is important to have a good supply of candles because they don't last long when you are using them every day.

As far as size is concerned, small candles are good for daily devotions but for major rituals, pillar sized candles should be used. The devotee might consecrate a candle to be used for a specific purpose, such as for Halloween or renewal of dedication promises. This will be put aside until it is time to use it again.

At the front of the altar on each side, there should be two medium or large black candles, and for devotional purposes, there should be a small black or red candle in front of the image of Satan. All other candles that are placed on the altar are optional.

INCENSE

When deciding on the type of incense to use, do some research to find out what the properties and purposes are for each type. Choose one based on the ritual or devotion you are doing. There are a variety of suitable ones to choose from, but under no circumstance should you use a type that is associated with Christianity as it would be disrespectful to Satan. The following list includes some good choices:

Cedarwood
Nag Champa
Patchouli
Musk
Dragon's Blood
Sandalwood
Amber
Opium
Jasmine

BELL

In your search for a bell you will come across many different kinds. Before purchasing one, make sure that it does not have symbols on it that you don't understand. I don't recommend getting a bell that would be used for mundane purposes such as the traditional school bell or dinner bell. Gongs can also be used and have a nice sound to them.

TREASURE BOX

This should be kept in front of the image of Satan. It contains the written promises made to Satan and personal offerings such as hair and nail clippings. It can also hold the money and coins given as offerings. The devotee may choose to draw a pentagram or symbols on the box to express their commitment and devotion. Images or words are also appropriate, if so desired.

OFFERING BOWL

This bowl is used primarily for offerings of food and drink. The devotee will most likely use a bowl made of glass, ceramic, or stainless steel because of their appearance and practicality. The best colour to use for this bowl is black, blue, or red.

BURNING BOWL

This is used primarily for burning the parchment paper containing written promises made to Satan. It is also used for burning certain offerings that have been placed on sigils such as blood, tears, and semen.

The bowl should be made of a material that will not burn or break, such as stainless steel, and it should be big enough to hold a fire safely. The devotee can decorate the bowl.

RITUAL KNIFE

This knife is for cutting the palm to obtain blood for an offering or promise ritual. It should be kept clean and not used for anything else. A lancet may also be used.

DIVINATION ITEMS

Items that the devotee uses for communicating with Satan can be placed on the altar. This can include Tarot cards, pendulum, or black mirror. Items used for other divination purposes should be kept elsewhere.

WALL

On the wall above the altar should be a pentagram or Sigil of Baphomet. Because of its importance in Satanism, it should be at eye level, the focal point of your rituals and devotions. If the devotee chooses to have other images over the altar, they should have a special meaning or importance and be placed either beside or below the pentagram. These can be sigils, images of Satan, prayers, or words of devotion.

OFFERINGS

OFFERINGS are an important part of a devotee's Satanic practice. An offering is given out of love and devotion to Satan. Although they are part of many rituals, the kind of offering discussed here is given on its own or as part of a devotion. It is freely given without any expectation of getting something back in return.

When deciding on an offering, the devotee thinks carefully about what they want to give and why they want to give it. The intent is most important and it must come from the heart. If you want to give Satan something but are not sure if it is acceptable, ask him, and wait for his response. He will show you in some way.

When the devotee has decided on an offering, they should invest their time, energy, and money into getting the best offering they can. If it is an alcohol drink, go to the store and choose one that you might not have tasted before. You don't have to buy an overly expensive drink but don't buy something cheap either. This is the Prince of Darkness, so think about what you would serve him if he was sitting at your dining room table and then go one step further. If you are giving a candle, make sure it doesn't have any dents or scratches on it and that you dress it with a special oil first.

The most powerful offering is what you give of yourself such as blood, hair, and tears. These must be given with a deeper reverence as they contain your life force, your DNA, and so it is a more serious offering. It will strengthen your connection to Satan and it will make it much easier to communicate with him.

The frequency in which a devotee gives an offering to Satan is up to them. You can give one every day, once a week, or once a month. For daily offerings, you may burn an incense stick or light a devotional candle. For weekly offerings, you may want to give food or money. Don't let anyone try to force you into giving an offering that you are not yet ready to give. If it is not freely given, it is not a true offering.

When giving an offering to the different aspects of Satan, the devotee must consider what would be most appropriate. For example, if you are giving an offering of roses to Lucifer, you might choose the colour blue but if giving them to Satan, you might choose black or red.

Creative endeavors can also be given as offerings such as paintings, poems, and music. Before beginning a work, the devotee must tell Satan that they are doing it for him and concentrate on him during the process of making it. Depending on what is promised, the finished product might be placed on the altar or sent out into the world for Satan to use in his own manner.

The devotee will give the offering in a reverent manner. They will bow and then hold the offering up in the air and say, "Satan, I give you this offering of____, may you accept it from me." Then they will place the offering in front of the image of Satan or set it aflame in the burning bowl. Ashes from burnt offerings can be buried or thrown into a lake or stream.

BLOOD

Blood is the most powerful of offerings. When the devotee offers their blood to Satan in this way, it is different than when it is used for dedications or promises. This is because it is given out of love and reverence for Satan with no other purpose. It is done by making a small cut on the palm or by piercing the index or middle finger with a lancet or pin. The blood is then put on a piece of parchment paper and offered to Satan. It is set aflame and placed in the burning bowl. If the devotee wishes to use their menstrual blood, the blood should be new, taken on the first or second day of their period and then offered in the same way.

DRINK

If the devotee wants to give a drink offering, it should be something special such as alcohol or goat's milk and bought for this purpose. If you decide to give a portion from what you also plan on drinking, the offering must be given first, as soon as you open the bottle, and then you can drink the rest. This is to show Satan respect and reverence. Once it is placed in the offering bowl, it is put on the altar in front of the image of Satan. It must be removed within 24 hours, and then disposed of at the special spot outside that you have designated for offerings.

CANDLES

A candle can be given as an offering if it is burned for this purpose. The devotee may choose to draw or carve a pentagram, sigil, or words of adoration on it. While placing it in front of the image of Satan, tell him that it is being given as an offering to him. Burn it for a few minutes each time you go to the altar.

HAIR

Hair is a very powerful offering. It is a part of you and contains your DNA, (for nuclear DNA it needs the root). If you decide that it is something you want to give, expect to feel Satan's presence strongly that day. To give an offering of hair, make sure it is freshly washed and brushed and then after it is dry, snip a few strands from underneath the back of your head with a pair of scissors or you can pull out a couple of strands with your fingers. After offering it to Satan, place the hair in the treasure box during your devotional.

FLOWERS

Fresh flowers are a nice offering to give to Satan. Make sure to purchase a vase that can be kept on the altar and wash it after every use. The flowers you give should be ones that you are drawn to and feel 'right' about offering. Dark colours are the most suitable. Be sure to take proper care of them, and don't let them wither while on the altar. Dispose of the flowers where you normally place your offerings.

NAIL CLIPPINGS

If you want to give nail clippings as an offering, use nails that are cut strictly for this purpose. It is disrespectful to use nails from a trimming. They would be considered leftovers from your normal hygienic routine and so they would not be considered an offering. During your devotional, offer the clippings to Satan and then place them in the treasure box.

FOOD

When food is being offered to Satan, it should either be prepared just for this purpose or it should be the first cut or serving before the rest of the food is eaten. Meat can be offered before it is cooked. The food is to be placed in the offering bowl and placed in front of the image of Satan. It is to be left for no longer than 24 hours and then it is to be disposed of outside your home.

TEARS

If the devotee would like to offer their tears to Satan, it is best to give the tears that are released from emotions during prayer or while listening to devotional music and thinking about Satan. These have the best intentions and are the most respectful. It is done by collecting the tears on your finger and placing them on parchment paper. They are then offered to Satan and the paper is set aflame and placed in the burning bowl. They can also be placed in the treasure box.

SEMEN OR VAGINAL FLUID

If semen or vaginal fluid is offered, it should be a result of masturbation done for this purpose. The devotee will masturbate in a reverent manner, and at the time of ejaculation, they will concentrate all their energy on Satan and will release onto parchment paper. Satan's sigil or a pentagram may be drawn on the paper beforehand but it is not necessary. The semen or vaginal fluid is then offered to Satan and the paper is set aflame and placed in the burning bowl.

INCENSE

If you want to give incense as an offering during your devotions, choose an incense and tell Satan that you are burning it in his honour. Let the stick burn in its entirety.

MONEY

Money that is offered to Satan can be given both in coins and bills. The amount is determined by the devotee when they feel drawn to give or as part of a promise that has been made during a ritual. The money is placed in the treasure box or on the altar in front of the image of Satan. It can only be used for Satanic items or can be saved up for something declared in writing through an agreement that was made with Satan. Always ask Satan's permission before using the money.

SATANIC ANOINTING

To be anointed means to be chosen by Satan. This can happen before birth or later in a person's life. If Satan has chosen you it means that you are special to him, and he has set you apart from the rest of humanity.

If a devotee has been chosen, Satan will let them know at some point in their life, often in childhood when they start to feel his presence or experience his signs. He will manifest in the way they will recognize him. This might be as the familiar devil figure, especially if the person is from a Christian background, or he might appear as a raven or serpent. The means in which he will do this are vast but the common ones are through dreams, signs, and manifestations. He might use words or images but either way, the person will have an inner knowing that it is Satan. His essence will become familiar, and the energy in the atmosphere will change. There will be no doubt that it is the Horned One of the Sabbath that has come for a visit.

Satan will give his chosen ones a mark and it could be physical, spiritual, or both. The physical mark might be a small blemish on the skin or it could be an unusual high intelligence, intuition, or psychic ability. The spiritual mark can't be seen by humans but spiritual entities can see it, and they know that the person is off limits to them. Satan also gives his chosen ones his Black Flame. This will help them on their spiritual path and to develop knowledge and wisdom. It will transform them to become more Satanic in nature.

It is important to note that just because someone might call themselves a Satanist, it doesn't mean that they have been chosen by Satan. It could be wishful thinking on their part. These people will most likely leave Satanism at some point after deciding it is not the path for them.

Another way that Satan anoints a person, is when he gives

them a special task. This could be one job and take a short period of time or it could be an assignment that takes many years. A person might be called to a life of service to Satan where they will be led to devote their life to him completely. In this case, the desire to serve him will be overwhelming and the devotee will know in their spirit that this is what they were born to do. If they try to take another path, they will always be led back, and Satan will be there waiting.

The most common definition of the word anointed is the act of being touched with oil or other substance in a religious ceremony. This can be done by the priest or priestess of a coven or if the devotee is a solitary practitioner, they can do it themselves during a ritual or devotion. The devotee will anoint themselves in Satan's name. They can use oil, perfume, or ointment but it must be bought for this purpose and consecrated to Satan before it is used. They can also use their own blood.

The anointing is best done at the beginning of the day, which can be day or night depending on the person.

To anoint yourself do the following:

1. Close to the end of your devotion or ritual, get the substance you wish to anoint yourself with and take a small amount with your middle finger.

2. Draw a pentagram on your forehead with the substance. Visualize Satan standing before you, his energy penetrating your third eye as he draws the symbol on your forehead and anoints you. Say:

> "I anoint myself in the name of Satan
> and in his name, I go forth."

If you are wearing any Satanic jewelry, use whatever might be left on your finger and anoint it as well.

3. Spend a few minutes in prayer, dedicating the day to Satan and asking his blessing on your endeavors.

4. Continue with your devotion or ritual. It is done.

PRAYING TO SATAN

As a devotee of Satan, prayer should be the most important part of your spiritual practice. This is because talking to Satan is core to having a strong connection with him.

The devotee desires more than anything to spend time alone with Satan. Nothing compares to feeling his ancient presence, his powerful energy in the air and sitting in silence experiencing his essence. Then there are times you can't remain silent. You want to tell Satan what he means to you and thank him for all he has done in your life. There are no rules in Satanism that say a Satanist must pray a certain amount of times a day, but the devotee will be drawn to pray often.

Satan doesn't demand that his followers pray to or worship him, but he does welcome it and does listen. To those who are true devotees, he will respond if he chooses to, but it is important that you be open to receiving his signs and wonders.

If you haven't already, you will probably come in contact with people who will tell you that prayer is a Christian thing to do and that it is not Satanic. Yet if one was to research prayer, they would find that people have been praying to their gods and goddesses since the beginning of time. Prayers have been found from the earliest civilizations such as Mesopotamia, Sumeria, Ancient Greece, and India. And considering that the Ancient Egyptians were very devotional, it is highly likely that people had been praying to Set, an early manifestation of Satan, way before anyone would have started to pray to the Abrahamic god.

It is important to arm yourself with knowledge. Research this subject, so that if anyone tries to dissuade you from praying to Satan, you will be able to inform them of the facts. That all forms of devotion and worship including hymns, psalms, mantras, prayer beads, and the writing of proverbs existed many years before Christianity.

Some have a negative view of prayer because of what they might have seen as a child, but praying to Satan is not the same as what happens in a Christian church or Islamic mosque. There is no begging out of guilt, shame, or fear and there is no worry of eternal punishment. Now if the devotee has done something they believe might have displeased Satan, they will take a close look at their actions or inaction and do everything they can to make things right. If they have fallen off their path, they will get up and start moving forward once again, and will make a promise to Satan that they will not make the same mistake. Satan respects this much more than he would if someone were grovelling while prostrating themselves.

When you pray to Satan, it is best to be at your altar away from distractions, so you can light a candle in reverence. Prayer can also be done outdoors at a quiet spot away from crowds. You can talk out loud or in your mind, he can hear you either way. Satan might also let the devotee know when he wants to talk to them. He might give you that inner nudge letting you know it is time to go to your altar or to go outside for a walk to spend time with him. Those are special times.

There is no special position that a devotee must be in to pray. It is most respectable to bow but it is also acceptable to stand or to sit in front of the altar if you will be praying for a long time. If you want to kneel, that is acceptable also and it shows Satan that you truly mean what you say and that you revere him. It is putting your ego aside and being humble before the one you call Master or Lord.

It is extremely important when you pray, that you mean everything you say. Do not ask Satan for something that you are not sure you want, and don't make promises you don't know if you can keep. It is best to wait until you are ready, then to make a promise and then break it. If you are saying a prayer written by someone else, make sure you agree with everything written, if not, omit the parts you do not agree with and add your own words where you feel appropriate.

HOW TO PRAY TO SATAN

These are the steps to take if the prayer is not being included in a formal ritual or devotion.

1. Go before the altar. Light the candle that is in front of the image of Satan.

2. Bow your head.

3. Take a couple of minutes to contemplate what you are going to say. Imagine Satan's magnificent presence in front of you.

4. Say what comes from your heart.

5. At the end of your prayer say, "Nema."

6. Snuff out the candle.

SATANIC BAPTISMAL RITE

This rite is for the new Satanist, especially those who have come from a Right Hand Path religion such as Catholicism.

To be done on a New Moon.

Items needed:
    White robe or white outfit
    Black robe or black outfit
    Glass of water
    Bucket

1. Take a ritual bath.

2. Put on the white garment.

3. Bow before the altar.

4. Light the candle in front of the image of Satan and then light the two black candles at the front of the altar.

5. Burn Sandalwood incense.

6. Take a deep breath, and for a couple of minutes focus on your breathing. Contemplate on what this baptism means for you. Prepare your mind and spirit.

7. Ring the bell 9 times.

8. Take the dagger and draw a pentagram in the air 3 times. Say, "Hail Satan," each time.

9. Say:

"Lord Satan,
I come before you this night
with the intention of shedding the old,
and beginning a new life on your infernal path.
I ask that you baptize me.

114

Cleanse me from all things holy.
Vanquish all previous sacraments and words placed upon me.
Break all ties that I may have with the Abrahamic god
and with all religious institutions.
Set me apart.
Fill me with your essence,
so I may become a child of darkness.
It will be done."

10. Take off the white garment. Visualize pulling everything off of yourself that was religiously done to you as a child, and anything of the white light religions that you participated in as a teenager or adult and throw it down. Stamp on it. Destroy it. Picture any guilt, shame, or fear that you might still have, fall off you and break into pieces on the floor. Take a deep breath and feel the weight fall off your shoulders. Say:

"With the shedding of this garment,
I renounce all previous religious affiliations.
I renounce all previous sacraments and
dedications to other gods.
I renounce the Abrahamic god in all its forms.
I renounce all white light religions.
I replace guilt with honour.
I replace shame with pride.
I replace fear with confidence.
I am free."

11. Stand naked in front of the altar. Take a deep breath as you contemplate your new freedom. Take the glass of water. Bend over the bucket that you have placed on the floor. Pour the water over your head. As you do this, say:

"I am baptized in the name of Satan."

12. Now put on the black garment. Visualize darkness enveloping you. Take a deep breath as it overpowers all your senses. Imagine Satan standing in front of you, his hand on your head. As he infuses you with his energy, see

the currents going through the top of your head, down and throughout your body. Your body starts to tingle. Accept it. Take a deep breath and feel yourself being devoured by the darkness. Say:

> "I have become one with darkness.
> I am reborn.
> As a child of the dark,
> I have been clothed in wisdom.
> Anointed with Satan's infernal essence,
> I now move forward on my new path,
> with Satan as my God."

13. Sit on the floor and remain in quiet meditation for about 15 minutes or for as long as you feel is needed.

14. Stand. Place the dagger on your heart and say:

> "So it is done."

15. Ring the bell 9 times.

16. Snuff out the candles.

DEDICATION RITUAL

To dedicate yourself to Satan.

To be done on a New Moon. The devotee must fast for 12 hours before the ritual, unless they have a medical condition that prohibits it.

Items Needed:
  Large pillar black candle (Dedication candle)
  Parchment paper
  Pentagram necklace or ring bought for this purpose
  Ritual drink
  Dragon's Blood ink

1. Take a ritual bath.

2. Bow before the altar.

3. Light the candle in front of the image of Satan and then light the two black candles at the front of the altar.

4. Burn Nag Champa incense.

5. Take a deep breath, and for a couple of minutes, focus on your breathing. Contemplate on what this dedication means for you. Prepare your mind and spirit.

6. Ring the bell 9 times.

7. Take the dagger and draw a pentagram in the air 3 times while saying:

"Hail Satan."

8. Say:

"Lord Satan,
I come before you this night to dedicate myself to you.
I have thought about this strongly, and make this decision

with a sound mind, and with my whole heart and soul.
This is my choice,
and I have not been influenced by anyone.
I welcome the venom of the Serpent,
and the mysteries of the Raven.
I will drink from your chalice,
the liquid of transformation.
I will serve you when circumstances are good
and when they are bad.
This is my path,
my destiny.
I understand that my life will never be the same.
I know I can never turn back,
nor would I want to.
You are my God,
and I will be loyal to you forever."

9. Light the dedication candle and place it in the middle of the altar.

10. Sit on the floor with legs crossed in front of the altar. Close your eyes. Visualize Satan in front of you. He has a chalice in his hand, and as he reaches out to give it to you, you take it. As you hold the chalice, think about what it symbolizes. When you are ready, drink, and as the metallic liquid warms your throat, you feel Satan's essence flow through all the parts of your body. Receive it, and know that you are now his.

11. Take the parchment paper and with the Dragon's Blood ink, write your promise:

Lord Satan,
I dedicate my mind, body, spirit, and soul to you.
I promise to serve you in this life and the life hereafter.
I believe in you,
and I will follow you and only you.
I will do your Will always.
I give you my eternal devotion.

May your darkness consume my spirit,
as you have my total allegiance.
Receive me as your child and devotee.
Nema!

12. Now read it out loud.

13. Take the ritual knife and make a small cut on your left palm. Put some of the blood on your index finger and sign your name under your promise. Then say:

"It is done."

14. Light the parchment from the dedication candle. Burn it in the burning bowl. (Make sure you keep an extra copy in your treasure box that you will read out loud each Halloween.)

15. Stand quietly for a few minutes and contemplate what you have done.

16. Take the pentagram necklace or ring. Put it on reverently. Say:

"With this necklace/ring, I pledge to serve you always. It is a symbol of my eternal dedication."

17. Pour some of the liquid from the chalice into the offering bowl. Say:

"Satan, I give this offering to you as a sign of my gratitude."

18. Drink the rest of the liquid.

19. Snuff out the dedication candle. (After the ritual, put it away till Halloween when you will renew your promise.)

20. Place the dagger on your heart and say, "So it is done."

21. Ring the bell 9 times.

22. Snuff out the candles.

HALLOWEEN RITUAL

To focus on all aspects of Satan.
To renew the devotee's dedication to Satan.
To make promises and set goals for the upcoming year.

To be done at midnight on Halloween.

Items Needed:
 2 Medium sized black candles
 2 Medium sized orange candles
 The dedication candle
 Parchment paper
 Ritual drink
 Sandalwood incense
 Halloween candy

Preparation: Place two orange candles on each side of the altar at the back. Place two black candles on each side of the altar at the front.

1. Approach the altar. Bow.

2. Light the black/red candle in front of the image of Satan.

3. Light the 4 corner candles, starting from the back and going clockwise.

4. Burn the Sandalwood incense.

5. Ring the bell 9 times.

6. Take the dagger and draw a pentagram in the air 3 times while saying, "Hail Satan."

7. Chant 3 times:

"Lord Satan, Primordial One.
Come this infernal night. Come! Come! Come!"

LVCIFER II · GUARDIAN OF THE CROSSROADS

8. Say:

"On this Halloween night, I call upon you, Lord Satan.
You are the Gatekeeper of the worlds,
and the Guardian of the crossroads.
The Creator and Destroyer.
The Prince of Darkness.
The Serpent in the garden.
Iblis, the God of fire and enemy of Allah.
That ancient Dragon called the Devil.
The Lord and master of all that is magical.
Pan, the Horned God of the Sabbath.
He that revealed himself as Melek Ta'us to the Yezidis.
Azazel, the Scapegoat of old.
Lucifer, the Lightbearer.
Set, the God of storms and disorder.
Satan, the adversary of the Abrahamic god.
Open my mind so that I may understand all your different
manifestations.
Appear to me as you Will.
I ask that you bestow upon me your characteristics.
Let me fly as the raven into your kingdom.
Help me to become Satanic,
for you are my God.
Nema."

9. Light the dedication candle. Say:

"I light this candle as a remembrance
of my dedication vows. I renew them
again this night. Here are my vows:[*]

"Lord Satan,
I dedicate my mind, body, spirit, and soul to you.
I promise to serve you in this life and the life hereafter.
I believe in you,
and I will follow you and only you.

---

[*]   The vows from your dedication ritual.

I will do your Will always.
I give you my eternal devotion.
May your darkness consume my spirit,
as you have my total allegiance.
Receive me as your child and devotee.
Nema!"

10. Make sure you have written down on parchment a list of your new goals and promises for the upcoming year. Say:

    "Lord Satan, for the upcoming year
    I promise to_____" (Read your list out loud).

11. Take the ritual knife and make a small cut on your left palm. Then with the index finger of your right hand, sign your name under the list. (Always make sure to keep a separate copy and place it in your treasure box.)

12. Light the parchment from the dedication candle. Burn it in the burning bowl.

13. Sit down in front of the altar and meditate for 15 minutes to a half an hour. Visualize yourself walking up to Satan. Bow. Ask him if he has anything to say to you. Spend time in silence and listen for his voice.

14. Take the chalice and pour some of the ritual drink into the offering bowl. Say:

    "I give you this drink as an offering, Lord Satan,
    as a token of my gratitude for all you have done."

15. Drink the remaining liquid from the chalice slowly.

16. Take the Halloween candy and place it on the altar in front of the image of Satan.

17. Say:

    "Thank you, Lord Satan, for being here this night."

18. Snuff out the dedication candle. (After the ritual, put it away till next Halloween when you will renew your promises once again.)

19. Place the dagger on your heart and say, "So it is done."

20. Ring the bell 9 times.

21. Snuff out the candles, this time going counter clockwise.

NINE DAYS OF SOLITUDE DEVOTIONAL

The Nine Days of Solitude Devotional is a retreat away from the mundane to spend time in devotion to Satan. This will help the Satanist strengthen their connection with Satan and give them a strong foundation on the path.

It can be started on any day of the week but must be continued for nine days in a row. It is to begin at midnight with the main ritual, then continue into the day with a meditation at sunrise, a contemplation at noon, and an offering at sunset.

It is ideal to be alone for the entire nine days, but if that is not possible, try to limit contact with people as much as you can. This is so you can give Satan your complete focus.

Items you will need:
  2 Black candles—one for each side of the altar*
  1 Red candle—to be placed in front of the image of Satan
  Ritual knife/lancet to use for the blood offering
  Ritual drink
  Anointing oil
  Parchment paper
  Vase for flowers
  Magical journal bought for this purpose
  9 items to be given to Satan as an offering each night

Offerings:
  Day One - Hair
  Day Two - Flowers
  Day Three - Fingernail clippings

---

*   These must be new and bought specifically for this devotional.

Day Four - Alcohol
Day Five - Tears
Day Six - Coins
Day Seven - Blood
Day Eight - Food
Day Nine - Goat's milk

Nine sticks of incense:
Day One - Cedarwood
Day Two - Nag Champa
Day Three - Musk
Day Four - Dragon's Blood
Day Five - Amber
Day Six - Patchouli
Day Seven - Opium
Day Eight - Jasmine
Day Nine - Sandalwood

SOLITUDE DEVOTIONAL
DAY ONE

Midnight

1. Bow before the altar.

2. Light the two black candles at the front, one on the right side and one on the left.

3. Light the red candle in front of the image of Satan.

4. Burn the Cedarwood incense.

5. Ring the bell one time.

6. Take the dagger and make a pentagram in the air. Do this three times while saying:

> "Hail Satan."

Then say:

> "In the name of Satan, I begin the first day
> of the nine days of solitude."

7. Take a deep breath, then let the air out slowly. Raise your hands at your sides and say the following invocation:

> "Lord Satan...
> Your power is beyond all power.
> No one dares to think they can exceed it.
> You were the first entity in existence,
> and the master of all.
> The Prince of Darkness.
> The Bearer of Light.
> Come, Lord Satan.
> Come!"

8. After a few minutes of silence, bow your head and say the following prayer:

> "Lord Satan...
> You are my God and master.

I seek you genuinely and with everything that I am.
I wish to know you intimately and without boundaries.
You are the only one with whom I want to commune.
You have led me to freedom,
and now I have power over fear.
I ask you to teach me,
guide me in all knowledge.
Initiate me,
and surround me with your fire.
Purify me,
and banish anything that is not of your kingdom.
Test me,
to reveal my true intentions.
No longer do I care what any man or woman thinks of me,
for I carry your strength within.
You have bestowed upon me your Black Flame,
so I belong to you.
Lord Satan, be with me this night,
and may I partake of your mysteries.
Nema!"

9. Now read the text out loud:

"Through all things, I am.
I am the gracious God.
The one that burns pure fire.
I am inviolate.
Tread lightly when you first walk on my path.
Know my strength.
I am power itself.
All who deem themselves worthy are not worthy.
I only call a select few.
Those dear to my heart.
Watch for me,
for I will manifest.
My incense will burn high.
No one takes from my power unless I Will it so.
People try to reach me but I am above them.

Perform your dance,
and I will come.
In the desolate places,
you will find me.
Burn candles in my honour.
Sing to me,
and I will listen.
Jump in celebration,
for I am near.
My chosen ones know my voice.
Don't call to me to appear in circles.
Can't you see I am Will itself?
I will cover you in darkness.
Find your home with me.
Hail my name.
I am the Adversary.
I am the Dragon.
I am the Serpent."

10. Take some time to contemplate what you just read, then say your own words of devotion to Satan.

11. Now take the chalice filled with the ritual drink, raise it in front of the image of Satan. Say:

"Lord Satan, I raise this chalice in your honour."

Then pour half of the liquid into the offering bowl saying:

"May this drink symbolize my eternal dedication to you."

Raise the chalice once more and say:

"As I drink from this chalice, may your essence enter my body and transform me as I commune with you."

Now drink, making sure to consume the remainder of the liquid.

12. Close your eyes and take a few minutes to feel the liquid as it slides down your throat and into your body. At the same time, visualize Satan pouring his essence into you.

You begin to feel warm and tingly as it merges with your body and spirit.

13. In closing say:

> "I give this day to you, Lord Satan.
> As each minute passes, may my connection
> with you grow stronger. Nema!"

14. Snuff out the candles.

Sunrise

15. Go before the altar. Bow.

16. Light the red candle in front of the image of Satan and then say the following chant:

> "O Devil! O Devil!
> You have called unto me.
> I am here. I am here.
> Waiting for thee to come.
> O Devil! O Devil!"

17. Sit on the floor and perform the following meditation:

Visualize yourself walking down a deserted road. There is a gentle breeze, and clouds begin to appear in the east covering the sun from view. As it becomes dark, you come to a crossroads. In the middle stands a figure with long black hair, wearing a black leather trench coat. As you approach, you feel the energy shift and the temperature drops several degrees. You stop, and it feels as if your legs begin to extend beneath the dusty ground, rooting you in place.

You know that you have not come this way by accident. You have been called here.

Lightning flashes in the sky and you see that the figure has not moved since your arrival. You don't have to ask him who he is as you already know. A raven flies down from a nearby tree and lands on his shoulder.

"Which path do you choose?" Satan asks of you.

You have needed to make this decision, but fear has held you back.

It's time.

Satan points to one path and then he points to the other. In your mind, you see glimpses of each but the end is not revealed. Taking a deep breath, you make your choice and step forward.

Take as long as you need to allow yourself to experience what comes next.

18. Say a few words of devotion to Satan.

19. Now take the anointing oil and put a tiny bit on your middle finger. As you draw an inverted pentagram on your forehead say:

> "I anoint myself in the name of Satan."

20. Snuff out the candle.

Noon

21. Re-read the text that you read out loud during the midnight ritual. Let every word sink into your mind and contemplate its meaning. Then ask yourself the following questions and write your answers in your journal:

What does it mean to be inviolate?

Why do you think it's important to tread lightly when you first begin on Satan's path?

What does it mean that Satan is power itself?

Do you feel called by Satan? Why or why not?

How has Satan manifested to you? How do you respond?

Have you made it a part of your spiritual practice to dance or sing for Satan? Why do you think that it is important to him?

What other things could you do to show your devotion?

What does it mean to know Satan's voice?

Satan has made it clear that he doesn't like it when people attempt to call him into a circle. How will this affect your practice?

Satan states who he is quite clearly. What are your thoughts on this?

Sunset

22. Go to the altar. Bow.

23. Light the candle in front of the image of Satan. Say, "I come before you this night to give you honour."

24. Sit on the floor in front of the altar and say some words of devotion to Satan. Spend some time in meditation.

25. Stand and say the following affirmation:

> "I believe in Satan,
> the Adversary.
> I believe in the Dragon.
> I believe in the Serpent.
> I believe in all his manifestations.
> He deserves my devotion."

26. Pull out a couple of strands of hair from your head. As you place them on the altar say:

> "This hair is for you, Lord Satan.
> I thank you for everything you have done for me and
> for your presence in my life. Nema!"

27. Ring the bell one time.

Spend the rest of the evening in quiet contemplation.

DAY TWO

Midnight

1. Bow before the altar.

2. Light the two black candles at the front, one on the right side and one on the left.

3. Light the red candle in front of the image of Satan.

4. Burn the Nag Champa incense.

5. Ring the bell two times.

6. Take the dagger and make a pentagram in the air. Do this three times while saying:

> "Hail Satan."

Then say:

> "In the name of Satan, I begin the second day
> of the nine days of solitude."

7. Take a deep breath, then let the air out slowly. Raise your hands at your sides and say the following invocation:

> "Lord Satan, Ancient One.
> I call upon you this night.
> You are the ruler of this world,
> and the leader of your infernal kingdom.
> Come!
> Come!
> Come!"

8. After a few minutes of silence, bow your head and say the following prayer:

> "Lord Satan . . .
> You appeared to the Yezidi people
> in the image of a peacock.
> Melek Ta'us.

The Blue God.
You gave them your revelation, Al Jilwah,
through your messenger, Sheikh Adi.
It is my desire to learn from this sacred text,
and to know you better.
Your words are precious and give hope to many.
Not just to the people in days of old,
but in the here and now.
They have reached far and wide,
and are everlasting.
I ask that you be with me this night.
May I come to a greater understanding of who you are.
Nema!"

9. Now read the text out loud:

"I am the Lord Satan.
I bring war and desolation.
I bring joy and pleasures unseen.
You call me saviour.
I am not.
I am the supreme adversary to all who need to be saved.
Jehovah is my enemy.
All who worship him are indeed my enemies also.
I hate three things.
Come to me with a pure heart.
Falsehood will not be tolerated here.
My chosen ones will bow down in reverence.
I kneel to no one.
I am the mighty Satan."

10. Take some time to contemplate what you just read, then say your own words of devotion to Satan.

11. Now take the chalice filled with the ritual drink, raise it in front of the image of Satan. Say:

"Lord Satan, I raise this chalice in your honour."

Then pour half of the liquid into the offering bowl saying:

"May this drink symbolize my eternal dedication to you."

Raise the chalice once more and say:

"As I drink from this chalice, may your essence enter my body and transform me as I commune with you."

Now drink, making sure to consume the remainder of the liquid.

12. Close your eyes and take a few minutes to feel the liquid as it slides down your throat and into your body. At the same time, visualize Satan pouring his essence into you. You begin to feel warm and tingly as it merges with your body and spirit.

13. In closing say:

"I give this day to you, Lord Satan.
As each minute passes, may my connection
with you grow stronger. Nema!"

14. Snuff out the candles.

Sunrise

15. Go before the altar. Bow.

16. Light the red candle in front of the image of Satan and then say the following chant:

"Hail Satan! Hail Satan!
Truth and falsehood are known to you.
Beautiful Peacock God. Melek Ta'us.
Hail Satan! Hail Satan!"

17. Sit on the floor and perform the following meditation:

You are sitting alone under a tree. It is an extremely hot day and you have chosen a place in the shade to protect yourself from the sun. Men wearing white turbans and talking in a language you don't understand walk quickly past you. You know them to be the Yezidi people and you are in their homeland.

Feel the energy of this place.

People are running back and forth and you wonder what is going on. A child gives something to his father and he looks back in astonishment. He speaks to him, and you wish you could understand. A woman comes, takes his hand and leads him back the other way.

There is a tiny breeze and then you hear a soft voice.

"Melek Ta'us."

You turn around to see who whispered in your ear but there is no one there. A few minutes pass and you hear it again.

"Melek Ta'us."

It starts to rain and the sky becomes dark.

"Melek Ta'us." It is louder this time.

The ground begins to shake, and people are falling. You feel a strange sense of peace despite what is happening. Suddenly, the clouds disperse and the sun shines brighter than before. Out of the sky appears a large peacock. It lands, and everyone gets down on their knees, their faces against the ground. You have never seen anything so beautiful.

Its tail is at least a hundred feet long, and as he raises it up in the air, it opens like a fan and you feel like you are in the presence of royalty.

It is Melek Ta'us. The Peacock Angel.

He struts over to you. You are shaking as you are overcome with all kinds of emotions.

"Do you accept my covenant?" He asks you.

"Yes," you reply.

He places his head against your forehead. Light forms, and as it gets stronger, it begins to glow. The most amazing energy flows through your body. Your spirit is being transformed. Welcome it.

He whispers in your ear. Listen carefully and respond to him . . .

18. Say a few words of devotion to Satan.

19. Now take the anointing oil and put a tiny bit on your middle finger. As you draw an inverted pentagram on your forehead say:

> "I anoint myself in the name of Satan."

20. Snuff out the candle.

Noon

21. Go outside to the place where you usually leave your offerings to Satan. Take the offering that you made last night and leave it there.

22. Re-read the text that you read out loud during the midnight ritual. Let every word sink into your mind and contemplate its meaning. Then ask yourself the following questions and write your answers in your journal:

What does Satan mean when he says he brings war and desolation?

Looking at world events, past and present, can you see Satan's hand at work?

What kind of joy and pleasures does Satan bring?

What does Satan mean when he says that he is the adversary of all who need to be saved?

Is Jehovah your enemy? Why or why not?

What are the three things that Satan hates?

What does it mean to go to Satan with a pure heart?

Do you believe that you are a chosen one of Satan? Why or why not?

Do you bow to him? If not, why?

23. Go to the altar. Bow.

24. Light the candle in front of the image of Satan. Say:

    "I come before you this night to give you honour."

25. Sit on the floor in front of the altar and say some words of devotion to Satan. Spend some time in meditation.

26. Stand and say the following affirmation:

    "I walk the Satanic path.
    I reject all past beliefs.
    The truth has been found by me.
    No longer will I condone falsehood and lies.
    I worship the Lord Satan."

27. Take the newly cut flowers that you bought that day, and as you place them on the altar say:

    "These flowers are for you, Lord Satan.
    I thank you for everything you have done for me and
    for your presence in my life."

28. Ring the bell two times.

    Spend the rest of the evening in quiet contemplation.

DAY THREE

Midnight

1. Bow before the altar.

2. Light the two black candles at the front, one on the right side and one on the left.

3. Light the red candle in front of the image of Satan.

4. Burn the Musk incense.

5. Ring the bell three times.

6. Take the dagger and make a pentagram in the air. Do this three times while saying:

> "Hail Satan."

Then say:

> "In the name of Satan, I begin the third day
> of the nine days of solitude."

7. Take a deep breath, then let the air out slowly. Raise your hands at your sides and say the following invocation:

> "Lord Satan . . .
> Melek Ta'us. Peacock Angel.
> You are the God of the east.
> The God of the west.
> The God of the north and south.
> Your beauty shines throughout the cosmos.
> You give and take away.
> You appear to your chosen ones in many ways,
> and I ask if you would appear to me
> in the image that you so approve.
> I call upon you this midnight hour.
> Come!"

8. After a few minutes of silence, bow your head and say the following prayer:

"Melek Ta'us...
You are the Lord Satan.
The mighty one who is my God.
It is my Will to obey you in all things.
Test me,
so that I may be one with your desires.
I will do what you ask of me,
and I will be faithful to you always.
As I study your words,
I ask that you give me understanding.
Teach me what is below the surface.
The unseen.
The forbidden.
Reveal to me the truth of my past lives.
I wish to become all I was meant to be.
I thank you.
Nema!"

9. Now read the text out loud:

"I am Pan.
I am Melek Ta'us.
I am Satan.
Take risks for me as I have for you.
Behind the veil there are many battles.
One day it will be your time to see.
Nothing is as it seems.
I have told you this and many other things.
My words will guide you in this world and the next.
I will not carry you,
but I am with you.
You must walk yourself,
as it is your journey.
It does not matter where you live in this world.
I am with you.
I can hear you when you speak to me.
I care about what you say.
I am not your adversary.

I am your God.
I will reveal myself to you in due time.
Come and sit at my altar.
Prepare for what is next.
Things will not be easy,
but I am close.
Call upon me in time of need.
I am the Lord Satan."

10. Take some time to contemplate what you just read, then say your own words of devotion to Satan.

11. Now take the chalice filled with the ritual drink, raise it to the image of Satan. Say:

"Lord Satan, I raise this chalice in your honour."

Then pour half of the liquid into the offering bowl saying:

"May this drink symbolize my
eternal dedication to you."

Raise the chalice once more and say:

"As I drink from this chalice,
may your essence enter my body
and transform me as I commune with you."

Now drink, making sure to consume the remainder of the liquid.

12. Close your eyes and take a few minutes to feel the liquid as it slides down your throat and into your body. At the same time, visualize Satan pouring his essence into you. You begin to feel warm and tingly as it merges with your body and spirit.

13. In closing say:

"I give this day to you, Lord Satan.
As each minute passes, may my connection
with you grow stronger. Nema!"

14. Snuff out the candles.

Sunrise

15. Go before the altar. Bow.

16. Light the red candle in front of the image of Satan and then say the following chant:

> "Lord Satan, I hail thee.
> You have given me free Will.
> And for that I give you praise.
> Lord Satan, I hail thee."

17. Sit on the floor and perform the following meditation:

Take some time to consider the Satanic jewelry that you are wearing. It may be a Sigil of Baphomet, a pentagram, or a Sigil of Lucifer.

Meditate on it. Look at the symbol hanging from your neck and think about why you wear it.

Is it to show others that you are a devotee of Satan?

Is it because you want to feel Satan's presence close to you and by wearing the symbol it helps to do that?

Is it because you want to look upon it during the day to be reminded of what is truly important?

Is it to symbolize your dedication to Satan?

Whatever the reasons, it must be between you and Satan. In Al-Jilwah, Melek Ta'us instructed his followers to honour his symbol and his image. Do you do this?

Have you considered that you might be the only person that others might see wearing a Satanic symbol? Do you represent Satan well?

Close your eyes and visualize the symbols. Has wearing them changed you in any way? If so, how? Take your pendant or ring in your hand and feel the energy.

It is not just common jewelry that you are wearing, but important and powerful symbols of the Satanic religion.

Always, remember this.

18. Say a few words of devotion to Satan.

19. Now take the anointing oil and put a tiny bit on your middle finger. As you draw an inverted pentagram on your forehead say:

"I anoint myself in the name of Satan."

20. Snuff out the candle.

Noon

21. Go outside to the place where you usually leave your offerings to Satan. Take the offering that you made last night and leave it there.

22. Re-read the text that you read out loud during the midnight ritual. Let every word sink into your mind and contemplate its meaning. Then ask yourself the following questions and write your answers in your journal:

What risks has Satan taken for you? What about for humanity as a whole?

What are the battles that he speaks of?

Satan says that he will not carry you. What does he mean by this?

How often do you go before Satan's altar? After reading the text, will you make it a part of your practice to go more often?

How will you prepare for things to come?

Do you pray to Satan in the good times and the bad?

What are your thoughts on this text?

23. Go to the altar. Bow.

24. Light the candle in front of the image of Satan. Say:

   "I come before you this night to give you honour."

25. Sit on the floor in front of the altar and say some words of devotion to Satan. Spend some time in meditation.

26. Stand and say the following affirmation:

   "I believe in Pan.
   I believe in Melek Ta'us.
   I believe in Satan.
   I will stand for him in all things.
   I am a Satanist."

27. Clip a couple of your fingernails. As you place them on the altar say:

   "These fingernail clippings are for you, Lord Satan.
   I thank you for everything you have done for me and
   for your presence in my life."

28. Ring the bell three times.

   Spend the rest of the evening in quiet contemplation.

DAY FOUR

Midnight

1. Bow before the altar.

2. Light the two black candles at the front, one on the right side and one on the left.

3. Light the red candle in front of the image of Satan.

4. Burn the Dragon's Blood incense.

5. Ring the bell four times.

6. Take the dagger and make a pentagram in the air. Do this three times while saying:

> "Hail Satan."

Then say:

> "In the name of Satan, I begin the fourth day
> of the nine days of solitude."

7. Take a deep breath, then let the air out slowly. Raise your hands at your sides and say the following invocation:

> "Lord Satan . . .
> You are the God of initiation.
> Throughout the ages,
> you have led your people by word alone.
> Taught magick and forbidden knowledge.
> You are known by many names,
> and reveal your attributes in due time.
> You are the Prince of Darkness,
> and I call upon you this night.
> Come!"

8. After a few minutes of silence, bow your head and say the following prayer:

"Lord Satan . . .
As the years have passed,
you have spoken to me using many voices.
Unlike the Abrahamic deity,
you don't need a mediator.
You talk to your followers directly.
My greatest happiness comes from knowing
that I am loved by you,
and that you have chosen me from among a select few.
My purpose is to serve you.
I seek your wonders,
and receive your miracles when you choose to bestow them
upon me.
It is my desire to drink from your chalice.
To partake of your essence.
I adore you.
Nema!"

9. Now read the text out loud:

"Hail to me,
for I am the Lord Satan.
You come to me of your own free Will.
That is the only worship that I will accept.
Bring to me flowers and incense.
Sing to me ancient hymns.
I will teach you the hidden things,
for you are my chosen.
The days are long,
the nights are longer.
Dance for me in the moonlight.
Await my arrival.
Light your candles.
Chant my name.
Ask me what you may do for me,
for I am the master.
I have given you my Black Flame.
Use my gifts wisely,

146

and for my purposes.
Don't allow people to lead you astray.
Follow me only.
Do not call anyone God or Master but me.
Do my Will.
I am not here to answer your commands.
Seek me out.
Find me.
Sacrifice in my name,
and in my name only.
Listen for my words.
The time is near."

10. Take some time to contemplate what you just read, then say your own words of devotion to Satan.

11. Now take the chalice filled with the ritual drink, raise it to the image of Satan. Say:

> "Lord Satan, I raise this chalice in your honour."

Then pour half of the liquid into the offering bowl saying:

> "May this drink symbolize my
> eternal dedication to you."

Raise the chalice once more and say:

> "As I drink from this chalice,
> may your essence enter my body
> and transform me as I commune with you."

Now drink, making sure to consume the remainder of the liquid.

12. Close your eyes and take a few minutes to feel the liquid as it slides down your throat and into your body. At the same time, visualize Satan pouring his essence into you. You begin to feel warm and tingly as it merges with your body and spirit.

13. In closing say:

> "I give this day to you, Lord Satan.
> As each minute passes, may my connection
> with you grow stronger. Nema!"

14. Snuff out the candles.

Sunrise

15. Go before the altar. Bow.

16. Light the red candle in front of the image of Satan and then say the following chant:

> "Lord Satan, I call to thee.
> Your altar has been prepared for you.
> Come!
> I honour you this day.
> Lord Satan, I call to thee."

17. Sit on the floor and perform the following meditation:

Visualize yourself going to a desolate place. It could be under a bridge, by the railroad tracks, or a desert.

Explore your surroundings and let your senses feel every aspect of the atmosphere.

What do you see? Is there anything written on the wall or on the ground? There is a symbol that you recognize. What is it?

What do you smell? Is it a kind of incense?

What do you hear?

What does the energy feel like?

You whisper, "Satan."

"Satan."

"Satan."

A sudden breeze touches your skin and you close your eyes. You are aware of a strong energy behind you. Stand still as it surrounds you. Feel it. Remain like this for a couple of minutes.

You hear the fluttering of wings and you open your eyes. A raven lands on the ground in front of you.

Satan is here.

You ask him a question. Listen for his response. He gives you the answer to what you have wanted to know for a long time.

He shows you something. Respond to him appropriately.

18. Say a few words of devotion to Satan.

19. Now take the anointing oil and put a tiny bit on your middle finger. As you draw an inverted pentagram on your forehead say:

> "I anoint myself in the name of Satan."

20. Snuff out the candle.

Noon

21. Go outside to the place where you usually leave your offerings to Satan. Take the offering that you made last night and leave it there.

22. Re-read the text that you read out loud during the midnight ritual. Let every word sink into your mind and contemplate its meaning. Then ask yourself the following questions and write your answers in your journal:

Why is it important to go to Satan of your own free Will?

What are the differences between the worship that Satan accepts and the worship that the Abrahamic god demands?

What are some of the things that Satan has taught you?

Is chanting Satan's name a part of your spiritual practice? If not, do you plan on changing that?

What does it mean to have Satan as your master?

What is the Black Flame? How has it made a difference in your life?

Do you mistakenly call another entity "god?" If yes, how will you remedy this?

What does it mean to do Satan's Will?

Satan says to listen for his words. How does he communicate with you?

Sunset

23. Go to the altar. Bow.

24. Light the candle in front of the image of Satan. Say:

    "I come before you this night to give you honour."

25. Sit on the floor in front of the altar and say some words of devotion to Satan. Spend some time in meditation.

26. Stand and say the following affirmation:

    "I follow Satan of my own free Will.
    He is my only God.
    I serve him with everything that I am.
    I listen to his teachings.
    I cherish the Black Flame that he has given me."

27. Put the bottle of alcohol that you bought for this purpose on the altar, in front of the image of Satan. Say:

    "This alcohol is for you, Lord Satan.
    I thank you for everything you have done
    for me and for your presence in my life."

28. Ring the bell four times.

    Spend the rest of the evening in quiet contemplation.

DAY FIVE

Midnight

1. Bow before the altar.

2. Light the two black candles at the front, one on the right side and one on the left.

3. Light the red candle in front of the image of Satan.

4. Burn the Amber incense.

5. Ring the bell five times.

6. Take the dagger and make a pentagram in the air. Do this three times while saying:

> "Hail Satan."

Then say:

> "In the name of Satan, I begin the fifth day
> of the nine days of solitude."

7. Take a deep breath, then let the air out slowly. Raise your hands at your sides and say the following invocation:

> "Mighty Satan . . .
> You are the God of divination.
> You know the past,
> and what is to come.
> You are creator,
> and destroyer.
> You had no beginning,
> and you will have no end.
> I ask that you come and guide me this hour.
> Come! Come, Lord Satan!"

8. After a few minutes of silence, bow your head and say the following prayer:

"Lord Satan . . .
You are above all gods,
and I am honoured to be standing here before you this night.
You hate three things,
and what you hate I also hate.
I promise to keep your secrets,
and will suffer for your sake if you ask it of me.
Your path is beautiful,
yet I understand there is hardship.
I will continue to walk it,
no matter how difficult it becomes.
I will unite with those with whom you tell me to unite,
and I will follow your commandments and teachings.
May you manifest your Will in my life.
I reject all the teachings of the Abrahamic religions,
and I curse their god.
Lord Satan,
I walk through the gates.
As they close behind me,
I know that I am home.
Nema!"

9. Now read the text out loud:

"Chosen one.
Stand.
Call my name.
Come before me.
Sing.
I am your God.
My word will go forth to the mighty and the strong.
Do not fear.
It is not of me.
I am the Goat of the Sabbath.
The Earth is ruled by me.
Nothing can happen outside of my Will.
I have spoken the truth.
Ancient are my ways.

If you could only comprehend them.
Take care of my animals.
Take care of the sea.
Death will see you too soon.
Live every day as if it were your last one."

10. Take some time to contemplate what you just read, then say your own words of devotion to Satan.

11. Now take the chalice filled with the ritual drink, raise it to the image of Satan. Say:

"Lord Satan, I raise this chalice in your honour."

Then pour half of the liquid into the offering bowl saying:

"May this drink symbolize my
eternal dedication to you."

Raise the chalice once more and say:

"As I drink from this chalice,
may your essence enter my body
and transform me as I commune with you."

Now drink, making sure to consume the remainder of the liquid.

12. Close your eyes and take a few minutes to feel the liquid as it slides down your throat and into your body. At the same time, visualize Satan pouring his essence into you. You begin to feel warm and tingly as it merges with your body and spirit.

13. In closing say:

"I give this day to you, Lord Satan.
As each minute passes, may my connection
with you grow stronger. Nema!"

14. Snuff out the candles.

15. Go before the altar. Bow.

16. Light the red candle in front of the image of Satan and then say the following chant:

> "Hail Satan. Sabbatic Goat.
> Come forth!
> Teach me your unholy ways.
> Hail Satan. Sabbatic Goat."

17. Sit on the floor and perform the following meditation:

Hearing a rustling in the trees, you walk toward the most beautiful oak that you have ever seen. The bark is a dark brown without blemish and the leaves are dark green. A branch bounces up and down.

"Hiss."

A large snake slowly slithers down the tree and comes towards you. It is unlike any snake you have ever seen. It has intricate black markings on its smooth grey skin.

You walk backwards but it comes closer . . . closer.

"Let's discuss."

You stumble, and the serpent quickly catches you as it coils around your body.

"Hiss," he says by your ear. You are surprised that it calms you.

Everything goes out of focus around you except for the snake's glowing red eyes.

"Do you desire . . . the knowledge . . . of good . . . and of evil?"

You think about the stories you know about the Serpent and how a woman was asked the same question long ago.

"You must also choose . . . as an individual. Everyone must . . . eventually."

You contemplate the question.

"You cannot have one . . . without the other," he says, reading your mind.

"I choose knowledge," you say. "Of both." You understand that to have free Will, there has to be a choice, even though you might not like the choice.

The Serpent whispers in your ear. Listen carefully, and consider what he says to you.

He pushes his tongue between your lips. You feel it slither down your throat and into your chest. The middle of your chest begins to burn. He has placed his essence within you.

"Now go forth in knowledge."

Respond to the Serpent.

18. Say a few words of devotion to Satan.

19. Now take the anointing oil and put a tiny bit on your middle finger. As you draw an inverted pentagram on your forehead say:

"I anoint myself in the name of Satan."

20. Snuff out the candle.

Noon

21. Go outside to the place where you usually leave your offerings to Satan. Take the offering that you made last night and leave it there.

22. Re-read the text that you read out loud during the midnight ritual. Let every word sink into your mind and contemplate its meaning. Then ask yourself the following questions and write your answers in your journal:

When Satan calls you his chosen one, how does it make you feel?

In Satan's eyes, who are the strong and mighty?

Satan tells his chosen not to fear. Why do you think this is important to him?

If you fear something, what steps will you take to free

yourself from it?

Has Satan manifested to you as the Goat of the Sabbath? If yes, what were the circumstances?

What are some of the ways that Satan rules the Earth?

What do you believe is Satan's Will?

What are Satan's ways? What are you doing to understand them better?

What are Satan's animals? How do you think he wants you to take care of them?

What can you do to be more productive? What are the steps you plan to take to make sure that your life's purpose is fulfilled before you die?

Sunset

23. Go to the altar. Bow.

24. Light the candle in front of the image of Satan. Say:

    "I come before you this night to give you honour."

25. Sit on the floor in front of the altar and say some words of devotion to Satan. Spend some time in meditation.

26. Stand and say the following affirmation:

    "The Goat of the Sabbath is my God.
    I am his chosen one.
    I will not fear.
    I will take care of what he gives me.
    My life has purpose and I will live it to the fullest."

27. Put some tears on a piece of parchment paper. As you place them on the altar say:

    "These tears are for you, Lord Satan.
    I thank you for everything you have done for me and for your presence in my life."

28. Ring the bell five times.

   Spend the rest of the evening in quiet contemplation.

Midnight

1. Bow before the altar.

2. Light the two black candles at the front, one on the right side and one on the left.

3. Light the red candle in front of the image of Satan.

4. Burn the Patchouli incense.

5. Ring the bell six times.

6. Take the dagger and make a pentagram in the air. Do this three times while saying:

> "Hail Satan."

Then say:

> "In the name of Satan, I begin the sixth day
> of the nine days of solitude."

7. Take a deep breath, then let the air out slowly. Raise your hands at your sides and say the following invocation:

> "Lord Satan . . .
> Your symbols resonate with power.
> They are intricate and timeless.
> Appear to me as the peacock.
> Majestic and prideful.
> Beautiful beyond compare.
> This night, Lord Satan, come.
> Come! You are welcome here."

8. After a few minutes of silence, bow your head and say the following prayer:

> "Lord Satan...
> As the moon reaches its peak in the midnight sky.
> I join you on this infernal night.

I believe in you.
You are my God.
I honour your symbol and your image.
I will always observe the laws you have given.
Guide me in your ways.
Reveal to me your true servants,
as there are many people who like to deceive.
Show me the hidden things,
and I promise to keep them close to my heart.
I thank you for your presence.
I thank you for your wisdom.
I thank you for choosing me.
I wear your symbols with honour,
and to show my dedication to you.
You are my life.
Nema!"

9. Now read the text out loud:

"It is I, the Lord Satan, who has called you.
I am the Beast.
The Lord of the Apocalypse.
No battle shall ensue unless I Will it so.
I am the great Dragon of Chaos.
The mighty one.
I will shake the world.
Bring it to its foundation.
The leveling is not complete,
but in time it will happen.
Cry if you must,
but change is coming.
It is necessary.
There will be a purging.
There will be suffering.
Death will claim many,
but not all will be taken.
Climb the ladder of success.
It is my Will for you.

Cast down that which does not serve you.
Your freedom depends on it.
Burn for me incense.
Call to me by name.
The Beast is here.
The mighty Lord Satan."

10. Take some time to contemplate what you just read, then say your own words of devotion to Satan.

11. Now take the chalice filled with the ritual drink, raise it to the image of Satan. Say:

"Lord Satan, I raise this chalice in your honour."

Then pour half of the liquid into the offering bowl saying:

"May this drink symbolize my
eternal dedication to you."

Raise the chalice once more and say:

"As I drink from this chalice,
may your essence enter my body
and transform me as I commune with you."

Now drink, making sure to consume the remainder of the liquid.

12. Close your eyes and take a few minutes to feel the liquid as it slides down your throat and into your body. At the same time, visualize Satan pouring his essence into you. You begin to feel warm and tingly as it merges with your body and spirit.

13. In closing say:

"I give this day to you, Lord Satan.
As each minute passes, may my connection
with you grow stronger. Nema!"

14. Snuff out the candles.

15. Go before the altar. Bow.

16. Light the red candle in front of the image of Satan and then say the following chant:

> "Hail Satan! Hail Satan!
> You have come forth from the fire.
> The Beast! The Beast! You are the Beast!
> Blessed art thou.
> Hail Satan! Hail Satan!"

17. Sit on the floor and perform the following meditation:

> You have been called to a luscious forest. In the middle is an altar draped with a black cloth and on it are many black candles. In front of the altar is the Sabbatic Goat. He calls you by name and you approach him slowly.
>
> "Come, my chosen one."
>
> When you reach the altar, you kneel. Bowing your head, you wait for his next words. He tells you to stand. When you look up, you can feel him staring into your soul.
>
> He picks up the chalice from the altar. "Will you drink my elixir?"
>
> You answer, "Yes."
>
> "From this day forward you are to live out my Will."
>
> You take the chalice and drink. You feel stronger with a new sense of purpose. He whispers in your ear something that he wants you to do.
>
> Respond to him.
>
> As you leave the forest, you feel reborn.

18. Say a few words of devotion to Satan.

19. Now take the anointing oil and put a tiny bit on your middle finger. As you draw an inverted pentagram on your forehead say:

> "I anoint myself in the name of Satan."

20. Snuff out the candle.

21. Go outside to the place where you usually leave your offerings to Satan. Take the offering that you made last night and leave it there.

22. Re-read the text that you read out loud during the midnight ritual. Let every word sink into your mind and contemplate its meaning. Then ask yourself the following questions and write your answers in your journal:

What does Satan mean when he says he is the Beast and the Lord of the Apocalypse?

He says that a battle cannot begin unless he wants it to. How does this differ from the Abrahamic texts?

How does it make you feel to know that it is Satan who is in control?

Why does Satan want to shake the world and bring it to its foundation? What do you think this will look like?

What is the change that Satan is talking about?

What are the things that he will purge?

Why does Satan want you to be successful? What are your goals and what does success mean to you?

What are some of the things that you should cast out of your life? How could doing this bring you freedom?

Do you often burn incense for Satan? If not, will you start making this a part of your practice?

Sunset

23. Go to the altar. Bow.

24. Light the candle in front of the image of Satan. Say:

> "I come before you this night to give you honour."

25. Sit on the floor in front of the altar and say some words of devotion to Satan. Spend some time in meditation.

26. Stand and say the following affirmation:

> "I follow the Beast.
> The Beast who is Satan.
> The ruler of the Earth and of the cosmos.
> I will be loyal to him always.
> I will do everything in my power to be successful in all things.
> I learn from his teachings."

27. Choose some coins for your offering and place them on the altar. Say:

> "These coins are for you, Lord Satan.
> I thank you for everything you have done for me and
> for your presence in my life."

28. Ring the bell six times.

Spend the rest of the evening in quiet contemplation.

SOLITUDE DEVOTIONAL
DAY SEVEN

Midnight

1. Bow before the altar.

2. Light the two black candles at the front, one on the right side and one on the left.

3. Light the red candle in front of the image of Satan.

4. Burn the Opium incense.

5. Ring the bell seven times.

6. Take the dagger and make a pentagram in the air. Do this three times while saying:

> "Hail Satan."

Then say:

> "In the name of Satan, I begin the seventh day
> of the nine days of solitude."

7. Take a deep breath, then let the air out slowly. Raise your hands at your sides and say the following invocation:

> "Hail Lord Satan! Hail!
> I salute you this witching hour.
> O Horned One of the Sabbath.
> Come!
> You are the All-Begetter.
> The one to whom all things dance.
> Come, Lord Satan.
> You are the one."

8. After a few minutes of silence, bow your head and say the following prayer:

> "Lord Satan . . .
> As Pan you have ruled the wilderness.
> Roamed the forests throughout the world.
> Your devotees have built shrines in your honour.

They sing hymns to you in devotion.
Ruling the darkness,
the winter winds howl your name.
You are the Sabbath King,
the protector of animals.
As you play your pipes,
the creeping things dance.
I want to dance.
I want to dance to your tune.
O Lord Satan...
You have given me the freedom,
to be who I was meant to be.
I am grateful.
Allow me to feel your presence this night.
Fill me with your essence.
Nema!"

9. Now read the text out loud:

"My chosen,
don't rush your time with me.
Indulge in my presence.
Learn from me.
I have many things to teach.
My mysteries are sacred and only for a select few.
Only for those who receive my covenant.
Not all who call my name I receive.
I select my chosen ones wisely.
Those I call,
their soul is old.
They have wisdom beyond their earthly years.
I give them signs and manifest my being.
There should be no doubt in your mind if you are mine.
Create.
Become like me.
Don't waste precious time doing inconsequential things.
I am Iblis.
The pillar of fire.

I am Satan.
Adversary of the stagnant god.
Celebrate my victory,
for it is here.
Freedom comes at a cost,
but it has been gained.
No longer behave like you are still in chains.
Don't act like you can contain me.
False power is worthless.
I laugh at those who think they rule over me.
They will suffer at my hands.
As the day nears its end,
come to me.
Let us commune together."

10. Take some time to contemplate what you just read, then say your own words of devotion to Satan.

11. Now take the chalice filled with the ritual drink, raise it to the image of Satan. Say:

"Lord Satan, I raise this chalice in your honour."

Then pour half of the liquid into the offering bowl saying:

"May this drink symbolize my
eternal dedication to you."

Raise the chalice once more and say:

"As I drink from this chalice,
may your essence enter my body
and transform me as I commune with you."

Now drink, making sure to consume the remainder of the liquid.

12. Close your eyes and take a few minutes to feel the liquid as it slides down your throat and into your body. At the same time, visualize Satan pouring his essence into you. You begin to feel warm and tingly as it merges with your body and spirit.

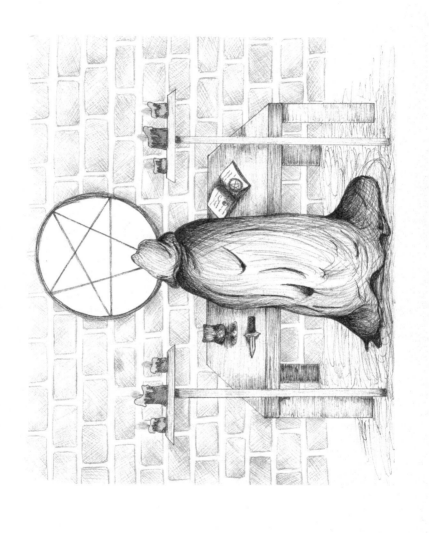

13. In closing say:

> "I give this day to you, Lord Satan.
> As each minute passes, may my connection
> with you grow stronger. Nema!"

14. Snuff out the candles.

Sunrise

15. Go before the altar. Bow.

16. Light the red candle in front of the image of Satan and then say the following chant:

> "Iblis, pillar of fire.
> You have destroyed the words of the Abrahamic god.
> You have brought disorder among man.
> Rise, Iblis! Rise!"

17. Sit on the floor and perform the following meditation:

Visualize yourself walking along a beach. You feel a cool breeze against your skin. It is midnight and the full moon is shining upon the lake. You stop to watch the waves hit the shore. They stop suddenly and the lake looks as if it has turned to ice. The swan that was swimming with its partner is gone. You look around and all is still. It seems as if time itself has stopped.

You try to walk but your feet feel heavy as if weights have been attached to the bottom of them to keep you in place. Looking up, you see a hooded figure walking towards you. His face is hidden. Your heart slows until you can't feel it anymore.

The figure comes closer and closer. He is wearing a black cloak and you think it is odd that it doesn't have any designs on it.

"I don't carry any symbols, nor do I need them. They are of humanity's design and are needed by them alone."

You are shocked that he read your mind. You try to

speak but the words don't come out.

"Shh!" He whispers as he places a long finger vertical to where his face should be.

Both of you stand there silently. You wonder who this figure is and why he has come to you.

"I am known by many names," he says slowly. "But you know me as Satan. Now come . . ." he reaches out his hand.

You remain still.

"It is your choice. You can give me your hand or you can turn and walk away."

What could he want to show you? You have seen his power—it stopped motion and time. Certainly, this has happened for a reason. You take one step forward, then another, and another. You reach out your hand and place it in his.

He says your name and then you know without a doubt that you have made the right decision. He leads you to the water, and as you put one foot down into the cold liquid, it suddenly becomes warm. He leads you further and further into the lake until the water reaches your neck. You stop.

"You doubt . . ." He says.

A part of you is afraid and wants to turn back, but deep down you want to experience what he has for you. Pushing your fear away with all your strength, you take a step forward as your mouth goes under the water. Once you are totally submerged, you look at the figure. His eyes are a deep blue with a tinge of red and they glow in the darkness. He tells you to close your eyes as he leads you further into the lake and you grasp his hand tighter.

"Open."

As your eyes slowly open, you see the most amazing place where you can do everything you have always wanted to do. You have seen it before in a dream that you remember from your childhood.

He points to the library. You go with him and he tells

you to pick out a book. You look across the shelves until you find one that you are drawn to. You pull it out and look at the cover. What does it say?

He tells you to open it. There is an illustration on the left side of the page. How does it speak to you? On the right side, there are a few words. He tells you that they are for you. What do they say? He tells you that you can take the book with you.

As you walk out of the library you can't stop thinking of the message that was in the book. He tells you that you can either leave and go back to the shore or you can stay and explore the underwater village.

What do you choose?

18. Say a few words of devotion to Satan.

19. Now take the anointing oil and put a tiny bit on your middle finger. As you draw an inverted pentagram on your forehead say:

"I anoint myself in the name of Satan."

20. Snuff out the candle.

Noon

21. Go outside to the place where you usually leave your offerings to Satan. Take the offering that you made last night and leave it there.

22. Re-read the text that you read out loud during the midnight ritual. Let every word sink into your mind and contemplate its meaning. Then ask yourself the following questions and write your answers in your journal:

What does it mean to indulge in Satan's presence?

Have you received Satan's covenant? Why or why not?

Would you describe your soul as being old? What are the reasons for your answer?

What does it mean to belong to Satan?

What are some of the ways you create? How can you become more creative?

What are some of the inconsequential things that you do, that you could stop doing, to better your life?

Has Satan ever manifested to you as Iblis, the pillar of fire?

What is Satan's victory and how has it affected your life?

What is one area of your life where you feel that you are not free?

Who are those who think they can rule over Satan?

How does it make you feel that Satan wants to commune with you?

Sunset

23. Go to the altar. Bow.

24. Light the candle in front of the image of Satan. Say:

   "I come before you this night to give you honour."

25. Sit on the floor in front of the altar and say some words of devotion to Satan. Spend some time in meditation.

26. Stand and say the following affirmation:

   "I am a chosen one of the mighty Lord Satan.
   I have received his covenant.
   I will make creativity a part of my life.
   I respect Satan and all his ways.
   I celebrate his victory."

27. Take some blood from your palm or finger and place it on the parchment paper. Place it in front of the image of Satan and say:

"This blood is for you, Lord Satan.
I thank you for everything you have done for me and
for your presence in my life."

28. Ring the bell seven times.

Spend the rest of the evening in quiet contemplation.

DAY EIGHT

Midnight

1. Bow before the altar.

2. Light the two black candles at the front, one on the right side and one on the left.

3. Light the red candle in front of the image of Satan.

4. Burn the Jasmine incense.

5. Ring the bell eight times.

6. Take the dagger and make a pentagram in the air. Do this three times while saying:

"Hail Satan."

Then say:

"In the name of Satan, I begin the eighth day
of the nine days of solitude."

7. Take a deep breath, then let the air out slowly. Raise your hands at your sides and say the following invocation:

"As the sun sets for the night,
and the moon rises in the sky,
Lord Satan, I call your name.
You are the Primordial One.
Mighty in power.
The Gatekeeper of all the worlds.
I ask if you would open the door to your kingdom,
so I can be in your presence.
O Lord Satan,
my God and Master."

8. After a few minutes of silence, bow your head and say the following prayer:

"Hail, Lord Satan!
You are above all gods.
Your power is above all power.
You call your chosen ones to solitude,
and you teach them in the darkness.
No one can lead another to you,
as they must approach you alone.
You reward those who are worthy,
and punish those who interfere with your Will.
You don't have a code of conduct, a book, or morals that must
be obeyed.
You have rendered useless the laws of the Abrahamic god,
and tore them to shreds.
You are desire, strength, lust, and pure Will.
And those who follow you must walk with honour.
Your reality cannot be denied.
Your truth will never cease.
No one can command or contain you.
If they try, you will pierce them with your fiery tongue,
and smash them to pieces in this world or the next.
I have dedicated my life to you.
You are my only God.
I want to learn about you intimately,
and spend eternity with you.
I ask if you would teach me this night.
Bestow upon me your wonders.
Nema!"

9. Now read the text out loud:

"As the clouds roll across the sky,
so does my presence across the earth.
I keep watch over my chosen ones,
they are never alone.
As the wind cleans the atmosphere,
I clean the soul.
I am a purging fire.
The God of the Sabbath.

Dance for me as the Witches do.
It is a time of celebration.
I am the Dragon,
and I bring gifts to those who are mine.
Come to the ritual chamber.
Drink from my chalice.
My elixir is good for the spirit.
Take.
Take.
Take.
Receive from me.
Don't turn away,
for I give good gifts and my manifestations are clear.
I will rise from the sea,
and will rip to shreds the order of the world.
Stand tall and watch.
Paint pictures.
Manifest my being.
For it is I who gave you life.
My name will be spoken throughout the earth.
The Lord Satan is here.
Choose.
Thrust your weapon into that which is stagnant.
Be strong.
Never lose your ground.
I walk among you.
My chosen will see me.
I am as the night.
The Prince of Darkness.
Lo and Behold it is I.
The winds are strong,
yet I am stronger.
I am the Mighty Lord Satan."

10. Take some time to contemplate what you just read, then say your own words of devotion to Satan.

11. Now take the chalice filled with the ritual drink, raise it to

the image of Satan. Say:

"Lord Satan, I raise this chalice in your honour."

Then pour half of the liquid into the offering bowl saying:

"May this drink symbolize my
eternal dedication to you."

Raise the chalice once more and say:

"As I drink from this chalice,
may your essence enter my body
and transform me as I commune with you."

Now drink, making sure to consume the remainder of the liquid.

12. Close your eyes and take a few minutes to feel the liquid as it slides down your throat and into your body. At the same time, visualize Satan pouring his essence into you. You begin to feel warm and tingly as it merges with your body and spirit.

13. In closing say:

"I give this day to you, Lord Satan.
As each minute passes, may my connection
with you grow stronger. Nema!"

14. Snuff out the candles.

Sunrise

15. Go before the altar. Bow.

16. Light the red candle in front of the image of Satan and then say the following chant:

"Prince of Darkness! Unholy one.
Rise from the abyss and join me here.
I wish to learn your mysteries.
Prince of Darkness! Unholy one."

17. Sit on the floor and perform the following meditation:

Walking down a wooden path, you notice that the trees on both sides are becoming dense. Very soon, you are surrounded by forest. It starts to get windy, and as the trees sway back and forth, you feel the first drop of rain. Lightning flashes in the distance, followed by a clap of thunder, and dark clouds begin to form overhead. You are alone and your heart begins to race. Wanting to go back from where you came, you turn around, but the path is gone and in its place is a crumbling brick wall. You have nowhere to go but forward. The rain hits you hard, and as the thunder gets louder you begin to run. You trip and fall, and as you get back on your feet you see lightning strike a tree in the distance and there is a loud crack.

The sky becomes dark and you can barely see the path divide into two. Lightning flashes and it reveals a building at the end of each path.

The building on the left side is a small cabin, humble in appearance. The wood is mouldy and a board is broken on the side, and it swings back and forth with the wind. The three steps to the red front door are slanted and are strewn with dark green leaves. Black liquid drips from the top step and onto the ground. The door has a tiny window that is covered by a dark blue curtain. As you look up, you see an unknown symbol on the very top of the cabin.

The building on the right is seven stories tall and made of fancy marble. Each level has two huge casement style windows that are lined with gold. One window is open on the top floor, revealing only darkness. There are ten cement stairs, draped in white carpet, that lead up to the veranda. The gold railings stretch out like arms at the bottom. The front door is a shimmering emerald and the window in the middle is outlined in gold. There is an unknown design on the inside of it.

You must choose one and you call out to Satan for guidance.

It seems like forever, but then you hear the familiar voice. "You must make the choice yourself."

Closing your eyes, you take a deep breath and hold it.

"Use wisdom, my devotee."

It is Satan.

As you let the air out of your lungs, you feel all doubt leave your mind. Standing tall, you take the first step on your chosen path. The rain stops, the air becomes still.

Reaching the building, you knock on the door and it opens wide. You enter . . .

Now—

Look closely at the figure who let you in. Are they human? Animal? Demon? Something else? Do they say anything to you?

Take a good look at everything around you, such as the walls, ceiling, furniture, decorations, and floor. What do you see? Does anything stand out to you?

Do you smell anything? If yes, what is it?

Do you hear anything?

There is a figure sitting at a desk at the back of the room. Walk up to them and introduce yourself. Do they tell you their name? Ask them if they have a message for you. Once they have given it to you, contemplate on it. If you have any questions, ask them.

After saying farewell, you take your leave. Opening the door, you see that the sky is clear and all is quiet. The brick wall is gone, and you walk down the path to where you first entered.

What have you learned? Did you make the right choice?

18. Say a few words of devotion to Satan.

19. Now take the anointing oil and put a tiny bit on your middle finger. As you draw an inverted pentagram on your forehead say:

"I anoint myself in the name of Satan."

20. Snuff out the candle.

21. Go outside to the place where you usually leave your offerings to Satan. Take the offering that you made last night and leave it there.

22. Re-read the text that you read out loud during the midnight ritual. Let every word sink into your mind and contemplate its meaning. Then ask yourself the following questions and write your answers in your journal:

How does Satan clean the soul?

When he says it is a time for celebration, what does he mean by this? What are some ways in which you can celebrate?

How is Satan's elixir good for the spirit?

What does Satan want you to take from him? What are some of the gifts that he gives to his chosen ones?

When he says that he will rip to shreds the order of the world, what does he mean?

Why does he want his devotee to paint pictures?

What are some of the ways in which Satan's name will be spoken throughout the world?

He says to thrust your weapon into what is stagnant. What is the weapon that he is talking about?

What are some of the ways that you have seen Satan?

After reading this text, what are your thoughts?

23. Go to the altar. Bow.

24. Light the candle in front of the image of Satan. Say:

    "I come before you this night to give you honour."

25. Sit on the floor in front of the altar and say some words of devotion to Satan. Spend some time in meditation.

26. Stand and say the following affirmation:

    "I honour Satan's presence in my life.
    I will dance for him in celebration.
    I spend time in the ritual chamber
    every day in devotion to Satan.
    I drink his elixir.
    I will speak his name throughout the world."

27. Make some food for this purpose only. Put it in a container and place it in front of the image of Satan and say:

    "This food is for you, Lord Satan.
    I thank you for everything you have done for me and
    for your presence in my life."

28. Ring the bell eight times.

    Spend the rest of the evening in quiet contemplation.

DAY NINE

Midnight

1. Bow before the altar.

2. Light the two black candles at the front, one on the right side and one on the left.

3. Light the red candle in front of the image of Satan.

4. Burn the Sandalwood incense.

5. Ring the bell nine times.

6. Take the dagger and make a pentagram in the air. Do this three times while saying:

> "Hail Satan."

Then say:

> "In the name of Satan, I begin the ninth day
> of the nine days of solitude."

7. Take a deep breath, then let the air out slowly. Raise your hands at your sides and say the following invocation:

> "Hail Satan! Hail Satan!
> You are darkness and light.
> The Baphomet manifested.
> You are known by many names throughout the world.
> From its beginning, you have been worshipped.
> I ask that you come.
> Come, Lord Satan! Come!
> Join me this night of all nights."

8. After a few minutes of silence, bow your head and say the following prayer:

> "Lord Satan . . .
> You have made your revelation clear to your chosen ones.
> To know you is pure ecstasy,

but for those who don't know you it is horror.
You make your enemies tremble.
They cannot speak your name for fear of you.
Those who worship you,
do so with a pure heart.
They desire to know you,
and approach you with the finest of incense.
There is no god but you,
and you manifest to your people.
Everything that is created is under you,
and you give guidance to those who ask with a sincere heart.
Your servants are few,
but they are the most devout of all.
Bowing down to you with an open mind,
ready to receive your truth.
You have chosen your priests and priestesses,
who serve you in secret.
They don't flaunt their position for the world to see,
but they know who they are.
You have called me to seek you only.
To devote my life to you alone.
I am here, Lord Satan.
Come!
I am waiting for you.
Nema!"

9. Now read the text out loud:

"Come . . . come.
See with my eyes.
Look at this world and beyond the veil.
Learn magick from me,
for I am the initiator.
Become the adept you were meant to be,
but don't get lost in the foolish systems created by man.
Call unto me,
for I will listen.
You have power within you.

It does not come from fancy words.
Change.
Go forth.
Make a difference for me,
for it is I who Wills it so.
I am the Black Mage.
All magick comes from me.
My eyes see the plentiful.
My eyes see the poor.
A soul is not judged by what it has or doesn't have.
Intent is key.
What you do with your power, I see.
Your actions will be judged.
Choose wisely.
Be loyal unto me."

10. Take some time to contemplate what you just read, then say your own words of devotion to Satan.

11. Now take the chalice filled with the ritual drink, raise it to the image of Satan. Say:

"Lord Satan, I raise this chalice in your honour."

Then pour half of the liquid into the offering bowl saying:

"May this drink symbolize my
eternal dedication to you."

Raise the chalice once more and say:

"As I drink from this chalice,
may your essence enter my body
and transform me as I commune with you."

Now drink, making sure to consume the remainder of the liquid.

12. Close your eyes and take a few minutes to feel the liquid as it slides down your throat and into your body. At the same time, visualize Satan pouring his essence into you. You begin to feel warm and tingly as it merges with your

body and spirit.

13. In closing say:

> "I give this day to you, Lord Satan.
> As each minute passes, may my connection
> with you grow stronger. Nema!"

14. Snuff out the candles.

Sunrise

15. Go before the altar. Bow.

16. Light the red candle in front of the image of Satan and then say the following chant:

> "Lord Satan, Great Dragon.
> Through synchronicities you reveal your Will.
> Your truth will be known throughout the world.
> Rise up!
> Lord Satan, Great Dragon."

17. Sit on the floor and perform the following meditation:

> A raven calls out in the distance, "Caw... Caw."
> Somewhere deep inside, your spirit senses who is coming. You hear him again, closer this time, and you rise, walk down the stairs and open the door. Looking up at the tree you see it there. It is the biggest raven you have ever seen. He twitches his head. His glowing eyes look at you and you feel naked, exposed as if he can see deep into your soul.
> He draws you like a powerful magnet and you take a step towards him.
> "Come." The word is a whisper inside your mind.
> Your heart begins to race as you take a few more steps forward. The sky becomes dark and you look up to see cumulus clouds as they slowly overshadow the moon till it is no longer in sight.
> "Closer."

The tree branches begin to move, yet the air is still. The aging leaves make a rustling sound, a chant to the majestic raven. You take another step, then another, and then you stop. Tilting your head back, your eyes gaze upon the one who has called you from your sleep.

The Primordial One.

You kneel and bow your head. You remain in that position for a few minutes until you feel something fall on your head. Reaching up, you grab the object. It is a feather.

"My gift to you. Keep it with you always."

Energy surges through your veins, and standing, you begin to sway in an unholy dance. You go deeper and deeper into your subconscious.

You are flying with the raven over a desert and he tells you to look down. What do you see?

Then with the blink of an eye, you are flying over a city. Two men are fighting. What else do you see and hear?

You are taken to a place with many trees and there is a swamp with dead fish floating on the top. How does it make you feel?

He takes you to a mountainous place. It is quiet except for the sound of birds chirping. You look down to see goats playing on the grass. He tells you to watch closely.

When you are back at the tree, the raven pokes out one of your eyes and replaces it with another. "From now on, see with my eyes."

18. Say a few words of devotion to Satan.

19. Now take the anointing oil and put a tiny bit on your middle finger. As you draw an inverted pentagram on your forehead say:

"I anoint myself in the name of Satan."

20. Snuff out the candle.

Noon

21. Go outside to the place where you usually leave your offerings to Satan. Take the offering that you made last night and leave it there.

22. Re-read the text that you read out loud during the midnight ritual. Let every word sink into your mind and contemplate its meaning. Then ask yourself the following questions and write your answers in your journal:

    Why does Satan want his devotee to see with his eyes?

    Have you asked Satan to teach you magick or have you relied on the words of people?

    How can you make a difference for Satan?

    What does he mean when he says that he is the Black Mage?

    In a world that bases worth on how much money one makes or how much material wealth they have, how does it make you feel knowing that these things are not important to Satan?

    What is meant by 'intent is key?' What are some of your intentions?

    Are you loyal to Satan?

Sunset

23. Go to the altar. Bow.

24. Light the candle in front of the image of Satan. Say:

    "I come before you this night to give you honour."

25. Sit on the floor in front of the altar and say some words of devotion to Satan. Spend some time in meditation.

26. Stand and say the following affirmation:

186

"I want to see with Satan's eyes.
All the things he has for me to see.
I will learn magick from him alone.
I choose to be an adept,
and I will make a difference for Satan.
I will be loyal to Satan always."

27. Put the container of goat's milk in front of the image of Satan and say:

"This goat's milk is for you, Lord Satan.
I thank you for everything you have done for me and
for your presence in my life."

28. Ring the bell nine times.

Spend the rest of the evening in quiet contemplation.

DAILY PRACTICE TO BECOME CLOSER TO SATAN

To be performed every day to strengthen the devotee's
connection with Satan.

Incense:
Sandalwood, Patchouli, Dragon's Blood, Cedarwood, or
Nag Champa.

Beginning of the Day

1. Before beginning your day, go before the altar.

2. Light the black/red candle in front of the image of Satan.
   Say:

   "Lord Satan, I light this candle in your honour."

3. Choose an incense from the above list. As you light it say:

   "Lord Satan, I burn this incense in your honour."

4. Take a couple of minutes to focus on the image of Satan.

5. Say the following prayer:

   "Lord Satan . . .
   You are the light and the dark,
   the yin and the yang.
   The Baphomet.
   I call upon you this new day,
   and I ask if you would help me to grow in wisdom—your
   wisdom, the knowledge of the ages.
   Teach me your magick and your divinations.
   If it be your Will,
   allow me to see with your eyes all there is to see.
   I long for your manifestations,
   and to know your hidden mysteries.
   As the Serpent in the garden you offered the fruit,
   and I take it freely.

It is my choice to follow you,
in all circumstances and situations.
No matter what might happen today,
I will remain by your side.
As the hours pass,
may there be many opportunities to learn more about you.
To know you in a more intimate and deeper way.
I give you this day, Lord Satan.
Nema!"

6. Spend some time in quiet contemplation.

7. Touch the top of the image of Satan with your fingertips. Close your eyes and imagine Satan's energy coming through the image and into your fingers. Say:

"Lord Satan, infuse me with your energy this day.
I wish to commune with you always."

8. Say:

"Thank you, Lord Satan for your presence.
I go forth to do your Will and my Will. Nema!"

9. Snuff out the candles.

Middle of the Day

10. Wherever you are, take a few moments to think about Satan. Say:

"Lord Satan, I am thinking of you.
You are the Ancient Serpent, the Primordial One.
Teach me your ways. Nema!"

End of Day

11. Before ending your day, go before the altar.

12. Once again, light the black candle in front of the image of Satan. Say:

> "Lord Satan, I light this candle
> as a sign of my eternal devotion."

13. Take a couple of minutes to focus on the image of Satan.

14. Say the following prayer:

> "As I close this day, Prince of Darkness,
> I thank you for everything you have done for me.
> For the signs that strengthened me,
> as I completed my tasks for the day.
> For revealing yourself in the little things,
> and giving me many teachable moments.
> You hold knowledge within your hands,
> free of all restraints,
> and with an aura of power beyond measure.
> You are unlike any other,
> there are no words that can adequately
> describe all that you are.
> I am honoured to be one of your chosen,
> and I am proud to call myself a Satanist.
> As I go to sleep,
> may I enter your presence.
> Nema!"

15. Spend some time in quiet contemplation. Listen for Satan's voice and be open to what he might say to you.

16. Then say the following chant:

> "Satan . . . Satan . . . Satan . . .
> Come, Lord Satan! Come this night. Come! Come!"

17. Take the dagger and place it over your heart. Say:

> "Lord Satan, I adore you with everything that I am.
> I make a promise this night—
> with you, Satan, as my witness.
> I promise to be the best I can be in every
> area of my life and to never lose hope.
> To keep going no matter what happens.

You are my everything, and I will live in your darkness
and your light forever. So, mote it be."

18. Snuff out the candles.

I encourage the devotee to change the prayers and chants
every day. You can use the ones that are in this book or
write your own.

For more information write to:
InSatansHonourPress@outlook.com

Made in the USA
Monee, IL
12 July 2020

36428865R00114